Cruelty as Citizenship

Forerunners: Ideas First

Short books of thought-in-process scholarship, where intense analysis, questioning, and speculation take the lead

FROM THE UNIVERSITY OF MINNESOTA PRESS

Cristina Beltrán
Cruelty as Citizenship: How Migrant Suffering Sustains White Democracy

Hil Malatino
Trans Care

Sarah Juliet Lauro
Kill the Overseer! The Gamification of Slave Resistance

Alexis L. Boylan, Anna Mae Duane, Michael Gill, and Barbara Gurr
Furious Feminisms: Alternate Routes on *Mad Max: Fury Road*

Ian G. R. Shaw and Marv Waterstone
Wageless Life: A Manifesto for a Future beyond Capitalism

Claudia Milian
LatinX

Aaron Jaffe
Spoiler Alert: A Critical Guide

Don Ihde
Medical Technics

Jonathan Beecher Field
Town Hall Meetings and the Death of Deliberation

Jennifer Gabrys
How to Do Things with Sensors

Naa Oyo A. Kwate
Burgers in Blackface: Anti-Black Restaurants Then and Now

Arne De Boever
Against Aesthetic Exceptionalism

Steve Mentz
Break Up the Anthropocene

John Protevi
Edges of the State

Matthew J. Wolf-Meyer
Theory for the World to Come: Speculative Fiction and Apocalyptic Anthropology

Nicholas Tampio
Learning versus the Common Core

Kathryn Yusoff
A Billion Black Anthropocenes or None

Kenneth J. Saltman
The Swindle of Innovative Educational Finance

Ginger Nolan
The Neocolonialism of the Global Village

Joanna Zylinska
The End of Man: A Feminist Counterapocalypse

Robert Rosenberger
Callous Objects: Designs against the Homeless

William E. Connolly
Aspirational Fascism: The Struggle for Multifaceted Democracy under Trumpism

Chuck Rybak
UW Struggle: When a State Attacks Its University

Clare Birchall
Shareveillance: The Dangers of Openly Sharing and Covertly Collecting Data

la paperson
A Third University Is Possible

Kelly Oliver
Carceral Humanitarianism: Logics of Refugee Detention

P. David Marshall
The Celebrity Persona Pandemic

Davide Panagia
Ten Theses for an Aesthetics of Politics

David Golumbia
The Politics of Bitcoin: Software as Right-Wing Extremism

Sohail Daulatzai
Fifty Years of *The Battle of Algiers*: Past as Prologue

Gary Hall
The Uberfication of the University

Mark Jarzombek
Digital Stockholm Syndrome in the Post-Ontological Age

(Continued on page 127)

Cruelty as Citizenship

How Migrant Suffering Sustains White Democracy

Cristina Beltrán

University of Minnesota Press
MINNEAPOLIS
LONDON

Published by the University of Minnesota Press
111 Third Avenue South, Suite 290
Minneapolis, MN 55401-2520
http://www.upress.umn.edu

Available as a Manifold edition at manifold.umn.edu

Contents

Introduction: Immigration, Latinos, and the Politics of the White Racial Imaginary

THE ANGER WAS SIMMERING long before Donald Trump. Before his pledge to build a wall at the southern border, before his call for a "deportation force" to round up unauthorized immigrants, before his proposals to deport Dreamers and defund sanctuary cities, before his "zero-tolerance" policy that put children in cages, nativist animosity was there.[1] Trump began characterizing migrants as agents of contamination long before he dubbed the COVID-19 pandemic "the Chinese virus"—and then "kung flu"—and exploit-

1. When referring to nativism, I am drawing on political scientist Cas Mudde's definition as "a xenophobic form of nationalism" that sees both nonnative persons and their alleged ideas as a threat to the nation-state's culture, security, and economic well-being. See Mudde, *The Far Right in America* (New York: Routledge, 2017), 89. Yet nativism is not merely prejudice. As Mudde illustrates, nativism reflects a set of beliefs regarding how the state should be structured, with nativists often seeking "a congruence of state and nation—the political and the cultural unit." See Uri Friedman, "What Is a Nativist?," *Atlantic*, April 11, 2017. As a form of boundary-based nationalism, nativism might initially appear to run counter to America's understanding of itself as a welcoming "nation of immigrants." But as scholars have long noted, nativist and right-wing politics have a long history in the United States. For example, particular definitions of whiteness have long shaped America's exclusionary immigration policies, with laws targeting Chinese, Catholics, and Jews as well as a variety of other racialized populations. See historian John Higham's *Strangers in the Land: Patterns of American Nativism, 1860–1925* (1955; repr., New Brunswick, N.J.: Rutgers University Press, 2002). Today, nativism is a core feature of the radical Right, with expressions of populism and authoritarianism tending to "pass through a nativist filter." See Friedman, "What Is a Nativist?"

ed an obscure public health law to deny refugees the ability to apply for asylum.[2]

Indeed, such vitriolic and dehumanizing rhetoric against migrants was already part of our national conversation. In calling Mexicans and other immigrants diseased, rapists, and criminals, Trump merely became the loudest voice with the ugliest, most unvarnished rhetoric.[3]

Indeed, for anyone paying attention, America has long been witness to a seemingly endless stream of xenophobic and racially charged statements, proposals, and policies targeting migrants—particularly Latinx migrants.[4] More than a decade before Trump's

2. See Julio Ricardo Varela, "As He Bungles This Crisis, Trump Turns to a Familiar Scapegoat: Immigration," *Washington Post,* March 23, 2020; "Donald Trump Calls Covid-19 'Kung Flu' at Tulsa Rally," *Guardian,* June 20, 2020; BBC News, "US–Mexico Border: Thousands of Migrants Expelled under Coronavirus Powers," April 10, 2020; Maria Verza and Ben Fox, "US Expels Thousands to Mexico after Largely Halting Asylum," AP News, April 9, 2020; Joel Rose, "Immigration Grinds to a Halt as President Trump Shuts Borders," NPR, March 18, 2020; Tal Axelrod, "Trump Threatens to Withhold Visas for Countries That Don't Quickly Repatriate Citizens," *Hill,* April 10, 2020; Adam Rogers, "Calling the Caravan's Migrants 'Diseased' Is a Classic Xenophobic Move," *Wired,* October 31, 2018.

3. For more on the history of race, immigration, and public health, see John Mckiernan-Gonzáles, *Fevered Measures: Public Health and Race at the Texas–Mexico Border, 1848–1942* (Durham, N.C.: Duke University Press, 2012), and Nayan Shah, *Contagious Divides: Epidemics and Race in San Francisco's Chinatown* (Berkeley: University of California Press, 2001).

4. In addition to using the national-origin term *Mexican* in this work, I also use the terms *Latino* and *Latinx* throughout. I use *Latinx* as the gender neutral and nonbinary alternative to *Latino.* However, when referring to Latinx subjects in plural terms, I will also use the term *Latinos,* as both terms refer to the diverse group of individuals living in the United States who trace their ancestry to the Spanish-speaking regions of Latin America and the Caribbean. For more on the political and theoretical possibilities of these terms, see Cristina Beltrán, *The Trouble with Unity: Latino Politics and the Creation of Identity* (New York: Oxford University Press, 2010); Ed Morales, *Latinx: The New Force in American Politics and Culture* (New York: Verso, 2018); and Claudia Milian, *LatinX* (Minneapolis: University of Minnesota Press, 2019).

election, congressman Steve King of Iowa suggested that the United States build a concrete border wall topped with wire to keep out migrants, stating, "We could also electrify this wire. . . . We do that with livestock all the time."[5] Six years later, King gave a speech comparing immigrants to dogs.[6] In 2010, Tennessee Republican Curry Todd likened undocumented immigrants to "rats [who] multiply." The next year, Kansas state representative Virgil Peck suggested that migrants be shot like "feral hogs" as a solution to America's "illegal immigration problem."[7] Echoing anti-immigrant politicians, conservative pundits such as Lou Dobbs, Pat Buchanan, Alex Jones, Rush Limbaugh, and Ann Coulter have built careers—and fostered an entire industry—based on attacking migrants, characterizing immigration as an existential crisis and encouraging the United States to pursue increasingly restrictive and punitive policies.[8]

Not only has immigration become increasingly partisan, dividing conservatives from liberals, but anti-immigrant sentiment has grown so intense that it fractures the American Right itself. This divide—between establishment conservatives who favor neoliberal forms of free trade dependent on an exploitable pool of immigrant labor and the more restrictive nativist wing—was on spectacular display at the 2018 Conservative Political Action

5. See Trip Gabriel, "A Timeline of Steve King's Racist Remarks and Divisive Action," *New York Times*, January 15, 2019.

6. Comparing the selection of "good immigrants" to dog breeding, King opined, "You want a good bird dog? . . . Pick the one that's the friskiest . . . not the one that's over there sleeping in the corner." See Glenn Thrush, "Rep. King Compares Immigrants to Dogs," *Politico*, May, 22, 2012; Stephen Pitti, "Congressman King, Cantaloupe Calves and Drug Mules," *Huffington Post Latino Voices*, July 25, 2013; P. J. Brendese, "Borderline Epidemics: Latino Immigration and Racial Biopolitics," *Politics, Groups, and Identities* 2, no. 2 (2014): 168–87.

7. Kevin Murphy, "Kansas Lawmaker Suggests Immigrants Be Shot Like Hogs," Reuters, March 25, 2011.

8. See the Anti-Defamation League Center on Extremism, "Mainstreaming Hate: The Anti-Immigrant Movement in the U.S.," November 2018.

Conference (CPAC), the annual gathering attended by conservative activists and elected officials from across the United States and, increasingly, Europe.[9] At the only 2018 CPAC panel dedicated to the topic of immigration, audience members "drown[ed] out panelists' presentation of the data about the benefits of immigration" with boos and jeers:

> During a heated question and answer session during the immigration panel, a man from Four Corners, Virginia, went on an extended diatribe about a Latino man who once crashed his car in front of his house. "I had to go down to court to testify, and I was the only white face in the crowd other than the lawyers being paid to translate for these people," he said. "You can go down to Four Corners Park and see obvious illegal immigrants defecating in the woods, fornicating in the woods, and on and on and on. These people are not the immigrants of the '20s and '30s. They will *never* be able to get good jobs here and be good citizens. Is *that* in your study?" . . .
>
> As David Bier, a policy analyst with the libertarian Cato Institute, attempted to lay out research proving that immigrants actually have lower crime rates than native-born Americans, contribute significantly to the economy and are assimilating just as well or better than past generations of immigrations, his fellow panelists derided his statements as "nutty" and angry audience members shouted him down. . . . Whenever Bier cited research to counter incorrect claims from his fellow panelists and the audience that recent immigrants are disproportionately criminal, are an economic drain on government or take several generations to learn English, he was met with vocal hostility.[10]

Insisting that today's immigrants are demographically and racially threatening ("I was the only white face"), disproportionately criminal, "obviously" illegal, impossible to assimilate, and spectacularly bestial ("defecating in the woods, fornicating in the woods"), it

9. As is widely known, the international movement of people has become a political flashpoint, in both the United States and throughout Europe. For the purposes of this book, my focus is on the U.S. and Latinx populations, particularly Mexicans and Mexican Americans.

10. Alice Ollstein, "Data Clashes with Emotion as CPAC Immigration Panel Goes off the Rails," *Talking Points Memo,* February 23, 2018.

became clear why CPAC organizers had elected to hold only one panel on the issue of immigration: additional events would have made the deep divide among conservatives even more conspicuous. Yet even at this single event, the split was as unmistakable as it was ontological. Both attendees and even some panelists at CPAC refused to accept not only the accuracy but the very *reality* of the facts and data presented by the Cato Institute, a libertarian think tank funded by the Charles Koch Foundation. In refusing to grant legitimacy to information and statistics widely understood to be accurate, participants embodied not only the disagreement but the deep incommensurability between certain segments of the GOP establishment and the nativist beliefs of the party's electoral base. Indeed, for a specific segment of politicians, pundits, activists, and voters, immigrants seem to serve as a kind of affective trigger, touching off paroxysms of rage and frustration regarding what they see as an existential threat to the United States and its economic future, sovereign integrity, and racial and cultural identity.

Given this dynamic, a number of questions come to the fore: Why has immigration—particularly from Mexico and Latin America—become such a potent and emotionally galvanizing issue for the American Right? What is driving the upsurge in anti-Latinx nativism at this historical moment? And why are Latinos (particularly migrants but often native-born Latinos as well) such an affectively charged population for political conservatives?[11]

11. Throughout this work, I generally refer to *migrants* rather than *immigrants.* The term *immigrant* generally refers to someone who has moved from one country to another with plans to relocate permanently. Technically, *immigrants* in the United States generally refers to legal permanent residents, those who hold visas, or those who have become U.S. citizens. By contrast, *migrant* is a broader term that refers to anyone who is in the process of relocating to another country as well someone who has already moved. The term is inclusive of refugees and asylum seekers as well as people who are still on the move or who have moved to a country but wish to eventually return to their home country. *Migrant* also makes no reference to legal status. For more on the distinctions between the two terms, see Adrian Vore, "'Immigrant' vs. 'Migrant': What's the Difference?," *San*

The intensity of nativist sentiment on the Right—their conviction that the United States faces an ever-worsening "crisis at the border" that must be confronted with increasingly draconian and violent measures—is made more striking by the fact that unauthorized immigration has been falling for more than a decade. In 2007, 6.9 million unauthorized Mexicans were living in the United States; ten years later, the number had fallen by 2 million. In fact, since 2015, Mexican migration to the United States has been net negative,[12] and Mexicans now compose fewer than half of all unauthorized immigrants living in the United States.[13] As Tomás Jiménez and Ana Raquel Minian point out, the incentives for Mexicans to go north had sharply declined even before the economic downturn in 2008 and *long* before Donald Trump pledged to build his infamous border wall.[14] Indeed, the comparatively steady size of the Mexican-origin U.S. population is maintained entirely by the birth of *U.S.-born* individuals.

The dramatic decline of Mexicans living in the United States has less to do with U.S. policies and border militarization than it does

---

Diego Union-Tribune, September 25, 2015. Moreover, as Alfonso Gonzales notes in *Reform without Justice: Latino Migrant Politics and the Homeland Security State,* when referring to Latinos, the term *migrant* better reflects the more "circular relationship" of migration from the Global South and the fact that many Latinx families have been migrating between nations for generations. Indeed, "in the case of indigenous migrants it could be argued that their history of circular migration within the Americas actually predates the modern nation state." See Gonzales, 184.

12. See Ana Gonzalez-Barrera, "More Mexicans Leaving than Coming to the U.S.," Pew Research Center, November 19, 2015.

13. Ana Gonzalez-Barrera and Jens Manuel Krogstad, "What We Know about Illegal Immigration from Mexico," Pew Research Center, June 28, 2019, and Jeffrey S. Passel and D'Vera Cohn, "U.S. Unauthorized Immigrant Total Dips to Lowest Level in a Decade," Pew Research Center, November 27, 2018.

14. See Ana Raquel Minian, "Looking South: The Development of Mexico's Emigration Practices," and Tomás Jiménez, "'This Too Shall Pass': Mexican-Immigrant Replenishment and Trumpism," both in *Democracy on the Line: Trumpism and the Latino Predicament,* ed. Phillip (Felipe) Gonzales, Mary Louise Pratt, and Renato Rosaldo (Santa Fe, N.M.: School of Advanced Research Press, forthcoming).

with simple demographics.[15] As Minian notes, since the 1970s, the Mexican government had adopted population-control policies that reduced Mexico's fertility rate.[16] The result has been that over the last fifty-odd years, the Mexican birthrate has dropped from almost seven children per mother to just over two, making today's potential migrant pool much smaller. As Peter Beinart observes, "even a strengthening U.S. economy hasn't lifted the numbers, because the young Mexican men who in past decades crossed the border today don't exist in the same numbers."[17] In other words, shifting economic opportunities in Mexico and the United States and changing fertility patterns—not "tough, zero-tolerance" policies—are what have reshaped patterns of migration. And while migrants are still coming from violence-plagued Guatemala, Honduras, and El Salvador to seek *legal* asylum, those three countries' populations are much smaller—*combined,* the three countries contain "about one-quarter as many people as Mexico."[18]

Alongside these demographic realities, polls also show that immigration is becoming a far less divisive issue for the *majority* of the U.S. population. The share of Americans calling for lower levels of immigration has fallen from a high of 65 percent in the mid-1990s to a record low of only 35 percent. The percentage of Americans saying immigrants "mostly help" the economy is at its highest point since Gallup began asking the question in 1993. According to a recent Pew Research poll, about two-thirds of Americans (62 percent) say that immigrants "strengthen the

15. Minian, "Looking South," 150.

16. Minian, 150. See also Anna Minian, *Undocumented Lives: The Untold Story of Mexican Migration* (Cambridge, Mass.: Harvard University Press, 2018).

17. Peter Beinart, "There Is No Immigration Crisis," *Atlantic,* June 27, 2018. For more on demographic and policy shifts within the Mexican nation-state, see Minian, *Undocumented Lives.*

18. Beinart, "There Is No Immigration Crisis."

country because of their hard work and talents."[19] Yet for nativist voters, the United States remains a nation besieged.[20]

Scholars and pollsters have long demonstrated that American politics has become increasingly polarized, with race, national identity, and immigration sharply dividing Democratic from Republican voters.[21] In their 2017 book *White Backlash: Immigration, Race, and American Politics,* for example, political scientists Marisa Abrajano and Zoltan Hajnal reveal how the issue of immigration has reshaped American politics: "white Americans who harbor anti-immigrant sentiments are much more likely than others to identify as Republican and favor Republican candidates." Millions of white Americans "who feel real anxiety about immigration" are drawn to the Republican Party because that is the political party "that has promised to ease such concerns."[22] Echoing Abrajano and Hajnal's findings, Lee Drutman of the Democracy Fund Voter Study Group found that "Trump's biggest enthusiasts within the party are Republicans who hold the most anti-immigration and anti-Muslim views, demonstrate the most

19. See Bradley Jones, "Majority of Americans Continue to Say Immigrants Strengthen the U.S.," Pew Research Center, January 21, 2019, and Jones, "Race, Immigration, and Discrimination," in *The Partisan Divide on Political Values Grows Even Wider* (Washington, D.C.: Pew Research Center, 2017).

20. To be clear, I'm not arguing that white nativism animates *all* criticisms of immigrant action. What this project seeks to understand is the particular logic of nativist subjects who are most deeply animated by anti-immigrant sentiments and who desire the intensification of violence against migrants.

21. See Ezra Klein, *Why We're Polarized* (New York: Simon and Schuster, 2020); Katherine Schaeffer, "Far More Americans See 'Very Strong' Partisan Conflicts Now than in the Last Two Presidential Election Years," Pew Research Center, March 4, 2020, and Norm Ornstein, "Yes, Polarization Is Asymmetric—and Conservatives Are Worse," *Atlantic,* June 19, 2014.

22. Marisa Abrajano and Zoltan Hajnal, *White Backlash: Immigration, Race, and American Politics* (Princeton, N.J.: Princeton University Press, 2015), 202.

racial resentment, and are most likely to view Social Security and Medicare as important within the Republican Party." According to Drutman, "almost a third of Trump voters (31.8 percent) responded with the strongest anti-immigration attitude on all three VOTER Survey questions."[23] Similarly, a study of the 2016 presidential election by Diana Mutz and published by the National Academy of Sciences found that Trump voters in 2016 were motivated less by economic anxiety than by fears of cultural displacement and the waning power and status of whiteness. For example, whites who said discrimination against white people is "a serious problem" were much more likely to favor Trump. Even more significantly, white voters who favored deporting immigrants living in the country illegally were 3.3 times more likely to express a preference for Trump than those who did not.[24]

Of course, policies that make life more violent and precarious for immigrants have long been a bipartisan affair.[25] Before Trump, Ronald Reagan, George H. W. Bush, Bill Clinton, George W. Bush, and Barack Obama all supported legislation and policies making migration a more punitive and perilous process.[26] Yet notwith-

23. Lee Drutman, "Political Divisions in 2016 and Beyond: Tensions between and within the Two Parties," report from the 2016 VOTER Survey, June 2017. The Democracy Fund Voter Study Group is a research collaboration of scholars and analysts that came together in 2016 to study the evolving view of the American electorate.

24. Diana C. Mutz, "Status Threat, No Economic Hardship, Explains the 2016 Presidential Race," *Proceedings of the National Academy of Sciences,* May 8, 2018.

25. See Daniel Denvir, *All-American Nativism: How the Bipartisan War on Immigrants Explains Politics as We Know It* (New York: Verso, 2020). Alfonso Gonzalez describes this bipartisan, pro-enforcement consensus as a form of "anti-migrant hegemony"; see *Reform without Justice,* 5.

26. The Immigration Reform and Control Act signed into law by Ronald Reagan in 1986 is often seen as pro-immigrant legislation, providing amnesty for more than a million undocumented immigrants and creating pathways to legalization that also allowed for family reunification. See Leo Chavez, *The Latino Threat: Constructing Immigrants, Citizens, and the Nation* (Palo Alto, Calif.: Stanford University Press, 2008), 7; Tanya Golash-

standing this long history of both parties criminalizing migration, a growing share of GOP politicians and voters appear to seek something beyond enforcement—they also desire visible displays of cruelty and suffering. Increasingly indignant over what they perceive as government tolerance for "illegal" immigrants, nativists take satisfaction in the violent targeting of those they feel have broken laws with impunity. For example, when the COVID-19 pandemic hit, undocumented workers suffered as much as (if not more than) anyone, yet Republicans inserted language into the federal government's $2.2 trillion aid bill barring $1,200 stimulus checks from going to not only undocumented taxpayers but anyone living in their households.[27]

Yet while numerous studies show that support for punitive immigration policies is central to why certain voters support Republicans more generally (and Donald Trump in particular), there is little in-depth analysis as to *why* this is the case. For example, while

---

Boza, *Immigration Nation: Raids, Detentions, and Deportations in Post-9/11 America* (Boulder, Colo.: Paradigm, 2012), 37–38. The law also sought to impose sanctions on employers, leading them to develop strategies to dodge federal oversight and consigning undocumented workers to a secondary labor market in which labor laws are routinely flouted. Employers devised workarounds that forced undocumented workers underground, making them more vulnerable. Ten years later, Bill Clinton passed the Illegal Immigration Reform and Immigration Responsibility Act, which made it more difficult for undocumented immigrants to adjust their status and become legal. Clinton also signed the Personal Responsibility and Work Opportunity Reconciliation Act, which sought to "end welfare as we know it." Part of this legislation also restricted *legal* immigrants' use of food stamps and Supplemental Security Income and barred *legal* immigrants from using Medicaid for five years after entry. See Chavez, *Latino Threat,* 7. Clinton's policies also led to a significant increase in the number of people being detained and deported in the United States. See Golash-Boza, *Immigration Nation*; Adam Goodman, *The Deportation Machine: America's Long History of Expelling Immigrants* (Princeton, N.J.: Princeton University Press, 2020); Denvir, *All-American Nativism.*

27. Julián Aguilar, "She's an Undocumented Immigrant, a Taxpayer and an Essential Worker. But She Won't Get a Stimulus Check," *Texas Tribune,* April 16, 2020.

Abrajano and Hajnal provide outstanding data analysis showing that anti-immigrant (and often anti-Latino) policy preferences play a significant role in the large-scale defection of whites from the Democratic to the Republican Party, the authors admit that "one question we have not answered is why so many white Americans feel threatened by immigration in the first place."[28] Claiming they are "largely agnostic about what it is that drives attitudes concerning immigrants," the authors acknowledge that there is a "wider range of mechanisms" that need to be looked at.[29] Ultimately, the authors simply note that "there is something significant about immigration itself that matters to white Americans when they make basic political decisions."[30]

This work seeks to identify that "something significant"—the assemblage of desires, anxieties, and aversions that generates intense anti-immigrant assertions and reactions from a certain segment of nativist voters. More specifically, how have America's racial and civic legacies helped create the conditions for the anti-migrant nativism we see today? Equally significant, what kind of world do nativists envision? What sorts of experiences or practices do nativists wish for? In sum, what constitutes the nativist imaginary?

And finally, while recognizing that anger, resentment, and fear are central to nativist sentiment, how should we understand the various *pleasures* that come with describing and enacting anti-migrant practices and policies? Why do certain forms of performative cruelty resonate with so many conservative voters? What sorts of civic satisfaction and meaning are made possible through anti-migrant speech and action? And what is the historical and political context for such delightful horrors?

28. Abrajano and Hajnal, *White Backlash*, 49.

29. Abrajano and Hajnal, 202, propose an immigration backlash theory that suggests changes in racial/ethnic demographics and media coverage as two mechanisms likely triggering public fears and anxieties over immigration.

30. Abrajano and Hajnal, 51.

It's my contention that making sense of contemporary anti-migrant sentiment requires confronting the violent and emotionally fraught history that political theorist Joel Olson refers to in *The Abolition of White Democracy* as the "democratic problem of the white citizen" and what W. E. B. Du Bois described as "democratic despotism."[31] Moving beyond studies that treat *whiteness* as a "neutral physical description of certain persons," this research approaches whiteness as a *political* project—a social relation that is both dynamic and historical, a "form of power that shapes the public sphere and is shaped by it."[32] Building on the insights of Olson and Du Bois, this book turns to works of political theory, history, cultural studies, and critical race studies (particularly scholarship in Latinx and whiteness studies) to examine how whiteness emerged as an ideology invested in the unequal distribution of wealth, power, and privilege—a form of racial hierarchy in which "the standing of one section of the population is premised on the debasement of another."[33]

31. Joel Olson, *The Abolition of White Democracy* (Minneapolis: University of Minnesota Press, 2004), xix; W. E. B. Du Bois, "The African Roots of War," *Atlantic,* May 1915.

32. Olson, *Abolition of White Democracy,* 9–10.

33. Linda Martín Alcoff, *The Future of Whiteness* (Cambridge: Polity, 2015), 15. Also see Olson, *Abolition of White Democracy,* xv. In addition to Alcoff and Olson, scholars of whiteness and white supremacy to whom I turn include W. E. B. Du Bois, *Black Reconstruction in America, 1869–1880* (1935; repr., New York: Free Press, 1998); Ida B. Wells-Barnett, *On Lynchings: Southern Horrors, a Red Record, Mob Rule in New Orleans* (1900; repr., Salem, Mass.: Ayer, 1990); James Baldwin, *Notes of a Native Son* (1955; repr., Boston: Beacon, 2012); Baldwin, *The Fire Next Time* (1963; repr., New York: Vintage, 1992); Lawrie Balfour, *The Evidence of Things Not Said* (Ithaca, N.Y.: Cornell University Press, 2001); David Roediger, *The Wages of Whiteness: Race and the Making of the American Working Class* (1991; repr., New York: Verso, 2007); Pierre L. van den Berghe, *Race and Racism: A Comparative Perspective* (New York: John Wiley, 1967); Charles Mills, *The Racial Contract* (Ithaca, N.Y.: Cornell University Press, 1999); George Lipsitz, *The Possessive Investment in Whiteness: How White People Profit from Identity Politics* (1998; repr., Philadelphia: Temple University Press, 2006); Nell Irvin Painter, *The History of White People* (New York: W. W.

In shifting attention to the political practice of whiteness and its relationship to anti-Latinx nativism, my work shares an impulse with the work of Olson and other political theorists who seek to theorize racial violence by "reversing the optic"—focusing attention not only on those who have been injured but on the political and affective desires and racial imaginaries of "those who *generate* injury."[34]

As Olson notes, racial oppression "makes full democracy impossible, but it has also made American democracy possible," meaning that American democracy "is not just a solution but a political problem" as well.[35] In this way, the United States can best be understood as "a white democracy, a polity ruled in the interests of a white citizenry and characterized by simultaneous relations of equality and privilege: equality among whites, who are privileged in relation to those who are not white."[36] As I discuss in the following pages, this collective understanding of the political meaning of whiteness evolved historically, marking a series of political choices that could have been otherwise. Such choices mean that for the majority of its history and until the passage of the Civil Rights Act of 1964, whiteness has come to function in the United States as a form of racialized *standing*, a status that "granted all whites a superior social status to all those who were not white, particularly African Americans."[37] And while communities of col-

---

Norton, 2011); T. R. R. Cobb quoted in William Sumner Jenkins, *Pro-Slavery Thought in the Old South* (Gloucester, Mass.: Peter Smith, 1960); and Noel Ignatiev, *How the Irish Became White* (New York: Routledge, 1995).

34. Hagar Kotef, "Violent Attachments," *Political Theory* 48, no. 1 (2020): 17. Other work in this vein includes Daniel Martinez HoSang and Joseph Lowndes, *Producers, Parasites, Patriots: Race and the New Right-Wing Politics of Precarity* (Minneapolis: University of Minnesota Press, 2019), and Lee Bebout, *Whiteness on the Border: Mapping the U.S. Racial Imagination in Brown and White* (New York: New York University Press, 2016).

35. Olson, *Abolition of White Democracy*, xv.

36. Olson, xv.

37. Joel Olson, "Whiteness and the Polarization of American Politics,"

or continually resisted the politics of white democracy, for generations, only a minority of white citizens acted politically against this form of racialized standing, making such opposition an atypical occurrence among most white citizens. Indeed, for much of its political history, the United States could be characterized as what the sociologist Pierre L. van der Berghe refers to as a *Herrenvolk democracy*—a regime that is "democratic for the master race but tyrannical for the subordinate groups."[38]

While many scholars have found the concept of Herrenvolk democracy useful, it has also sparked debates regarding how best to

---

Political Research Quarterly 61, no. 4 (2008): 704. Of course, as numerous scholars have noted, it was initially Reconstruction that marked the first national effort to truly challenge the politics of white supremacy and white democracy. Following the Civil War, the adoption of the Thirteenth, Fourteenth, and Fifteenth Reconstruction constitutional amendments marked the effort to graft the principle of equality onto the Constitution, with the federal government (not the states) put in charge of enforcement. These three constitutional amendments abolished slavery, guaranteed due process and equal protection of the law, and equipped Black men with the right to vote. Establishing the principle of birthright citizenship and guaranteeing the privileges and immunities of all citizens, the changes wrought by Reconstruction have been described as representing a "second founding of the United States." Unfortunately, Lincoln's successor, Andrew Johnson, along with many in the southern states, as well the Supreme Court all sought to actively undermine these newly established rights. A series of court decisions narrowed the rights guaranteed in the amendments; states actively undermined them; and by 1877, Jim Crow laws establishing racial segregation were being established and Herrenvolk democracy reestablished. See Du Bois, *Black Reconstruction in America*; Eric Foner, *Reconstruction: America's Unfinished Revolution, 1863–1877* (1989; repr., New York: HarperPerennial, 2014); and Foner, *The Second Founding: How the Civil War and Reconstruction Remade the Constitution* (New York: W. W. Norton, 2019).

38. Van der Berghe, *Race and Racism,* 18. A concept in Nazi ideology, *Herrenvolk* refers to the idea of a "master race," superior to other races and entitled to dominate and rule over their inferiors. Coordinated and imposed from above, der Berghe uses a comparative lens to consider the "paternalistic" and "competitive" modes of intergroup relations of various political regimes (including Brazil, Mexico, South Africa, and the United States).

understand white supremacy and its political effects. According to der Berghe, in Herrenvolk societies, a white minority maintains its privileged position by cultivating a sense of trust, solidarity, and equality among whites—an equality that stands in stark contrast to the despotic treatment meted out to nonwhite populations. By contrast, historian and American studies scholar David Roediger argues that while the early nineteenth century did see gains in political rights for poorer whites that were connected to the loss of rights by free Blacks, he also notes that "racism was not effectively linked to any significant social or political leveling among whites." Instead, "there was a simple pushing down on the vulnerable bottom strata of society, even when there was little to be gained, except psychologically, from such a push."[39] Roediger suggests that a more apt term than Herrenvolk *democracy* would be Herrenvolk *republicanism*—an ideology premised on a racialized belief in popular sovereignty and the rule of law, alongside a concomitant belief that the will of the people was being corrupted by those above and below. Feeling victimized by the rich and powerful while also feeling under assault from those below (often people of color), Herrenvolk republicanism had the advantage of reassuring white citizens fearful of downward mobility that "one might lose everything but not whiteness."[40] For Roediger, Herrenvolk *democracy* is the wrong term because racism did not actually lessen inequality among whites or dramatically improve their material lives. Thus Herrenvolk politics was not actually "democratic." In this way, we can see how Roediger conflates democracy with enhanced economic equality. Thus a more "democratic" society would be engaged in practices of "leveling" inequality.

While I agree with Roediger that there is an important relationship between democracy and economic equality, and that white subjects have often understood their citizenship as being

39. Roediger, *Wages of Whiteness*, 59.
40. Roediger, 60.

threatened from above and below, my point is that the practice of "pushing down on the vulnerable strata" was itself a practice of domination whose appeal was democratic. Regardless of class status and the various inequalities that existed between whites, white standing put the power to dominate into the hands of *all* white citizens. That is what I take to mean "democratic for the master race"—not that Herrenvolk democracy gave white citizens the experience of a more level, economically equal society but rather that the power to dominate (to "push down") was put in the hands of the many. Equally significant, in the United States, Herrenvolk democracy offered white citizens the material, psychological, and political satisfaction of being subjects protected by individual rights and the rule of law, while simultaneously allowing them the freedom to deny those same protections to those deemed nonwhite. Here my analysis draws on Charles Mills's account of a Herrenvolk ethic—an ethic that constitutes "a moral dividing line by which equality and subordination are reconciled."[41] For Mills, a Herrenvolk ethic means that members of a privileged population are "simultaneously committed to liberal egalitarianism *and* racial hierarchy."[42]

Initially premised on native dispossession and settlement and enriched through the stolen labor of human beings held as property, white democracy was *legally* sanctioned. Indian removal, chattel slavery, Black Codes, the Chinese Exclusion Act, segregated "Mexican schools" in Texas and across the Southwest, all-white police forces, racially exclusive housing covenants, Japanese internment, all-white juries, segregated facilities under Jim Crow in the South and Juan Crow in the Southwest—for the majority of U.S. history, white supremacy was not simply culturally acceptable but *legally* authorized. Racial discrimination was not de facto but

41. Roediger, 152.

42. Charles Mills, "White Right: The Idea of a *Herrenvolk* Ethics," in *Blackness Visible: Essays on Philosophy and Race* (Ithaca, N.Y.: Cornell University Press, 1998), 152.

de jure: white citizens had the legal right to deny equal rights to nonwhite citizens. Democratic for whites but tyrannical for subordinate groups, under Herrenvolk democracy, white citizens had access to the key components of constitutional liberalism defined by the rule of law and characterized by civil and political rights and civil liberties. Yet this form of liberalism was situated within a symbiotic relationship with white supremacy, in which the value of liberal citizenship was made manifest through the denial of equal rights and legal equality to nonwhite populations.

The tyrannical character of Herrenvolk democracy made it inevitable that white citizens would not simply come to expect and desire unequal applications of the law—many would seek to *be* the law, to replace the rule of law with their own actions and judgments and to see racial domination as a practice of freedom. In sum, Herrenvolk democracy in America was a form of democratic violence that begat violence and taught tyranny. Indeed, for the vast majority of our nation's history, the United States functioned via Herrenvolk logics—operating as a form of rule whereby the majority of white citizens gave each other permission to engage in and express public support for extralegal acts of violence against those deemed nonwhite. White violence—the lynching, raping, defrauding, murdering, and rioting that targeted nonwhite populations—was supported through both the explicit and tacit consent of local, state, and federal governments.

At the same time, white citizens saw themselves and their communities as both defenders and beneficiaries of liberal democracy. Indeed, as a space of both opportunity and racial exclusion, white democracy was often experienced by its beneficiaries as a form of freedom; for many white citizens, *whiteness as standing* worked to create a racialized sensorium that felt less like privilege and more like fairness. Spaces of racial homogeneity were normalized—territories, neighborhoods, schools, and workplaces were experienced as spaces of freedom where (white) mobility was encouraged, (white) equality was possible, and the rule of law and the values of constitutional liberalism prevailed.

Of course, the day-to-day reality of those spaces and communities was far from idyllic for anyone, and that fact—that white democracy's reality was messy, multifarious, and characterized by the failure of some to thrive—helps to both reinforce and obscure the reality of white privilege and white democracy. Lack of success among individual white citizens is read as proof of the system's fairness, reinforcing the conviction that one's achievements are personal and merit based rather than simultaneously historical, racial, and constituted by various forms of inequality. In this way, white citizens envision and experience opportunity and accomplishment not as racialized but as rightful and hard-won. Majority-white schools, neighborhoods, and community institutions were *made white* through violence; racialized exclusions; and the denial of equality, opportunity, and legal protection for nonwhite populations. Yet these racialized exclusions often went unacknowledged, constituted by a white supremacy that could remain unnamed amid forms of daily struggle and achievement that were also deeply felt. At the same time, Herrenvolk democracy was about more than unacknowledged and obscured exclusions or the embodied experience of white equality—it was also, importantly, about overt enactments of racial domination: the violent freedom to both wield and exceed the law.

In sum, by analyzing how white democracy has functioned as a political and participatory undertaking in the United States, my argument is not that racism has revealed the hypocrisy of a nation that espouses the ideals of freedom, equality, and democracy; rather, it's that American conceptions of equality, freedom, and democracy have historically been constituted *through* white supremacy. In other words, the *experience* of democracy, equality, and freedom cannot be fully detached from the political project of whiteness in the United States.

Along with scholars who argue that racial subordination "both constructs democratic ideals as well as violates them," this research shares the belief that racial oppression and American democracy have long been "mutually constitutive rather than antithetical" to one another.[43] Appreciating how race has fundamentally shaped our conceptions of sovereignty, tyranny, and the rule of law, this essay echoes Lisa Lowe's call for a "critical genealogy of liberalism" that explores how liberalism's abstract promises "were produced through placing particular subjects at a distance from the 'human.'"[44] Put somewhat differently, while critics like Adam Serwer have rightly argued that when it comes to the bond between Trump and his supporters, "the cruelty is the point," my claim is that such cruelty is not only an experience of community and delight; it's fundamentally a return to a particular *civic* experience.[45] The simultaneous experience of public happiness and racial tyranny is precisely what freedom and equality felt like in an earlier era of Herrenvolk democracy. In other words, whiteness needs to be reconceived not only as a discriminatory practice but as a particular type of *democratic* practice—a mass-based, participatory practice of exclusion and performative membership with one's fellow (white) citizens. For those invested in an ideology of whiteness, racial exclusion, violence, and domination *produce* a sense of membership, creating a commonsense understanding of community, opportunity, futurity, and possibility.

The passage of the Civil Rights Act of 1964 and the Voting Rights Act of 1965 dealt Herrenvolk democracy a seemingly lethal blow. Undercutting the legal bedrock of white supremacy, civil rights legislation marked the end of lawful racial discrimination and the sanctioned exercise of whiteness as standing; whites no longer have access to a state explicitly and officially committed to ensuring their personal standing as white. Yet *white democracy* persists even without legal imprimatur: whiteness continues to operate as "a form of social power," with many white citizens

43. Olson, *Abolition of White Democracy*, xv.

44. Lisa Lowe, *The Intimacies of Four Continents* (Durham, N.C.: Duke University Press, 2015), 167.

45. Adam Serwer, "The Cruelty Is the Point," *Atlantic*, October 13, 2018.

revealing "an interest in and an expectation of favored treatment in a polity whose fundamental principle is that all men are created equal."[46] Today, white democracy often functions as a system of "tacit and concealed racial privileges"—everyday practices that presume white advantage as the "natural outcome of market forces and individual choices."[47] At the same time, the persistence of white democracy is sometimes obscured by the simultaneous existence of both a growing, visible multiracial elite and a significant shift in how white identity is being understood and enacted. Let me take each point in turn.

Today, women and people of color make up more of America's political and cultural elite than in any time in our nation's history.[48] In 2008, Barack Obama became the first Black president; twelve years later, Democratic vice presidential candidate Kamala Harris became the first Black woman and the first Asian American to appear on a major-party ticket. Yet the growing diversity made visible by such barrier-breaking events exists alongside persistent racial disparities related to issues of poverty, policing, public health, wealth, incarceration, detention, education, and housing. Put somewhat differently, alongside the presence of an increasingly diverse population of professionals, politicians, academics, students, media figures, artists, and cultural workers, low-income communities of color continue to face a civic, economic, and political landscape characterized by forms of structural racism and economic inequality. Beyond examples of diversity in professional and elite spaces, we are also seeing the rise of a more heteroge-

46. Olson, "Whiteness and the Polarization of American Politics," 709.

47. Olson.

48. See John Laidler, "The Earnings Gap between Black and White Men," National Bureau of Economic Research, April 18, 2020; Thomas B. Edsall, "Black People Are Not All 'Living in Hell,'" *New York Times,* April 27, 2017; Jody Agius Vallejo, "Latino Elites Are Paying the California Dream Forward," *Conversation,* November 7, 2017; Jody Agius Vallejo, *Barrios to Burbs: The Making of the Mexican-American Middle Class* (Palo Alto, Calif.: Stanford University Press, 2012).

neous homeland security state. Increasingly, for aspiring working-class communities of color, one of the major paths into the middle class is through employment in the criminal justice system as well as in U.S. immigration and customs enforcement. Today, more than half of all Border Patrol agents are Latinx, while a growing number of police officers and prison guards are female, Black, and/or Latinx. Situated as both police and population, not only are African Americans and Latinos disproportionately harmed by carceral violence—far more likely to be detained, deported, incarcerated, killed, and injured—they are also crucial to the staffing, implementation, and legitimation of today's modern multicultural security state. In sum, the growing professional, ideological, and affective diversity of racialized and gendered populations is crucial to understanding how white democracy is a persistent yet evolving practice.

At the same time, as white democracy is simultaneously reinforced and reshaped by neoliberal multiculturalism, white identity is becoming increasingly heterogenous—more unstable, in flux, and divided than in previous eras. Today, the variability of white identity is visible in the growing rupture between white citizens who support the politics of white democracy and those increasingly appalled by racist and xenophobic appeals to whiteness.[49]

49. In saying this, I do not seek to ignore or downplay the implications of the ongoing shift in aggregate white partisanship. Trump was elected in 2016 because of the white vote. The *majority* of white men and women (58 percent) voted for Republican Donald Trump, whereas only 37 percent of whites voted for Democrat Hillary Clinton. See Alec Tyson and Shiva Maniam, "Behind Trump's Victory: Divisions by Race, Gender, Education," Pew Research Center, November 9, 2016. As Abrajano and Hajnal note, fully "91 percent of Republican identifiers are now white," while "slightly under half of all Democratic identifiers are now nonwhite." See Abrajano and Hajnal, *White Backlash,* 211; see also ANES (American National Election Studies), 2012 Time Series Study [data set], Stanford University and University of Michigan [producers], http://www.electionstudies.org/. Republican voters are mostly white,

The police killing of George Floyd, an African American man in Minneapolis, and the large presence of white people joining with communities of color to oppose racist policing and support the Black Lives Matter movement speak to the shifting and diverging politics of white identity.[50] In other words, the ability of white nativists to engage in Herrenvolk practices today is threatened not only by the growth of America's nonwhite population but *by the changing nature of white identity itself*.[51] Threatened not only by the presence of migrants and other people of color but also by a growing number of white citizens, nativists feel increasingly impeded and persecuted—making the pleasures of white democracy simultaneously more desirable and less acceptable. Today, for nativist voters drawn to the politics of whiteness, access to white-

---

while the Democratic electorate is far more multiracial. Such statistics speak to a troubling dynamic regarding whiteness, white identity, and practices of partisan and ideological identification.

50. See David Remnick, "An American Uprising," *New Yorker*, May 31, 2020, and Emily Stewart, "George Floyd's Killing Has Opened the Wounds of Centuries of American Racism," *Vox*, June 10, 2020.

51. While my analysis draws on Olson's regarding "the enduring problem of whiteness," I approach white identity in more dynamic terms, as another iteration of how race works—less as an identity that must simply be abolished and more as a "historically evolving identity-formation" produced in diverse locations and continually undergoing reinterpretation and contestation. In doing this, I make a critical distinction between an ideology of *whiteness* and *white identity*. As noted earlier, *whiteness* is a political project, an ideology invested in the unequal distribution of power and privilege. *White identity*, by contrast, is a characteristic of the self that has no biological or scientific foundation, a social identity that, as Bruce Baum insists, "comprises one of the myriad ways in which some people have come to understand themselves and their relations to others." Baum, "For Joel Olson, with Trayvon Martin on My Mind," *New Political Science* 36, no. 2 (2014): 242. And while whiteness is certainly constitutive of white identity, my analysis echoes Linda Martín Alcoff's in refusing the conflation of whiteness with white identity. Such an approach better equips us to consider how subjects who claim a white identity are continually engaged in practices that either sanction or repudiate whiteness. See Olson, *Abolition of White Democracy*, 66; Alcoff, *Future of Whiteness*, 15.

ness as standing appears both tantalizingly conceivable and legally (and often morally) disavowed. Citizens invested in the politics of whiteness—experienced as an increasingly unattainable promise—exist in a state of agitated and outraged betrayal, attached to forms of whiteness to which they feel entitled yet which they find increasingly difficult to attain.

It's this political environment that makes migrants a particularly potent target for nativist desire, rage, and fear. Indeed, migrants here in the United States (with or without legal sanction) represent the rare population offering nativists an administratively endorsed opportunity to access the power and pleasures of Herrenvolk democracy. As noncitizens, migrants are vulnerable to both state-sanctioned and extralegal practices of violence, enforcement, terror, exclusion, and removal—witnessed and enacted by a government and citizenry who claim democratic legitimacy by arguing that their actions are lawful, necessary, and authorized.[52]

For nativists who yearn for the freedom to police, punish, and exclude, targeting migrants makes them feel stronger, freer, and more agentic, transforming acts of racialized violence—whether people are committing, witnessing, or merely describing such acts—into feats of heroism, democratic redemption, civic engagement, and virtuous sovereignty.[53]

52. Of course, the policies, practices, and laws that nativists seek to impose on migrants are often *not* legal and have been subject to numerous challenges in the courts—see, e.g., Miriam Jordan, "Judges Strike Several Blows to Trump Immigration Policies," *New York Times,* October 11, 2019; Dara Lind, "Judge Tells Trump to Stop Sending Central American Asylum Seekers Back to Mexico," *Vox,* April 8, 2019. My point is less about the legality or legitimacy of the current laws governing immigration and more about the opportunity that noncitizens offer nativists to *invoke* the law in order to enact violence against what is generally perceived as nonwhite population. Akin to earlier assertions of whiteness as standing like state-sanctioned segregation, anti-immigrant practices offer nativists the increasingly rare opportunity to combine practices of overt racial domination with the invocation of law.

53. For a brilliant analysis of how American citizenship and conceptions of freedom, agency, and sovereignty have been shaped by narratives

At the same time, in taking up the question of white democracy and its relation to anti-migrant rhetoric and policies, this book shares the assessment of numerous Latinx and Indigenous scholars who believe that approaches to whiteness and racism in the United States too often rely on a Black–white binary that fails to address the history of other racialized and colonized populations. With the legacy of Mexican incorporation into the United States continuing to shape the current treatment and perception of migrants, I analyze white democracy through the fields of Chicano and Latinx studies, turning to the politics of Western expansion and the racial politics of the frontier to explore how this legacy of anti-Mexican violence helps to sustain today's rage-infused politics of American nativism.

Yet, in seeking to deepen our understanding of the relationship between Mexicans, migration, and the politics of whiteness, I also take seriously Latinos' complicated relationship to the politics of immigration and of whiteness. Mexicans, for example, have been enmeshed in a complex racial order based on not only a Euro-American racial order but a preexisting Spanish and colonial order that created complex racial dynamics in relation to questions of indigeneity and settlement. During early periods of colonial rule, some Mexicans participated in the enslavement of Indians, while others engaged in alliances with various tribal populations.

---

of victimization and vengeance, see Elisabeth Anker's *Orgies of Feeling: Melodrama and the Politics of Freedom* (Durham, N.C.: Duke University Press, 2014). For more on how such affective investments shape Mexican and Latinx populations, see Bebout, *Whiteness on the Border*; Arnoldo De León, *They Called Them Greasers: Anglo Attitudes toward Mexicans in Texas, 1821–1900* (Austin: University of Texas Press, 1983); David Gutiérrez, *Walls and Mirrors: Mexican Americans, Mexican Immigrants, and the Politics of Ethnicity* (Berkeley: University of California Press, 1995); María Josefina Saldaña-Portillo, *Indian Given: Racial Geographies across Mexico and the United States* (Durham, N.C.: Duke University Press, 2016); Chavez, *Latino Threat*; Nicholas Villanueva, *The Lynching of Mexicans in the Texas Borderlands* (Albuquerque: University of New Mexico Press, 2017); and Laura Gomez, *Manifest Destinies: The Making of the Mexican American Race* (2007; repr., New York: New York University Press, 2018).

Later, elite Mexicans exercised power and worked through the juries and territorial legislatures in the Southwest by claiming white status and distancing themselves from prior alliances with various tribal populations (such as the Pueblo in what would eventually become the state of New Mexico). The ambiguous racial position of Mexicans is a reminder that as a group, Latinos have been characterized at various times as white, nonwhite, Indigenous, Black, and not-Black, reflecting what Latino studies scholars have long noted: that Latinos "have no simple positioning in the U.S. racial order."[54]

Indeed, from the original U.S. Naturalization Law of March 26, 1790, that limited naturalization to "free white persons" to the Chinese Exclusion Act of 1882 to Mexican repatriation in the 1920 and 1930s, much of U.S. immigration law is a history of racialized assaults on particular segments of the American immigrant population. Such attacks on nonwhite immigrant populations help explain why the story of immigration has long been one of various populations trying either to claim whiteness and/or to assert themselves as not-Black in order to claim rights and standing and avoid the state-sanctioned violence and exclusions typically visited upon populations deemed nonwhite. Moreover, as Daniel Martinez HoSang and Joseph Lowndes insist, "while racial subordination is an enduring feature of U.S. political history, it continually changes in response to shifting social and political conditions, interests and structures. . . . Race performs dynamic and often contradictory work, continuing to produce hierarchy and exclusion while also articulating new forms of mobility and incorporation."[55]

54. See Bebout, *Whiteness on the Border*, 4. See also Gomez, *Manifest Destinies*; Victoria Hattam, *In the Shadow of Race: Jews, Latinos and Immigrant Politics in the United States* (Chicago: University of Chicago Press, 2007); and G. Cristina Mora, *Making Hispanics: How Activists, Bureaucrats, and Media Constructed a New American* (Chicago: University of Chicago Press, 2014).

55. See HoSang and Lowndes, *Producers, Parasites, Patriots*, 6.

In other words, while Latinos have often been victims of white supremacy and white democracy, some have striven to claim whiteness, seeking the privileges and pleasures of a polity that denies rights and dignity to those deemed nonwhite.[56]

Like HoSang and Lowndes, I approach race and the politics of whiteness and white identity as more protean categories than generally acknowledged. Indeed, I see the internal diversity and racial indeterminacy of Latinos as making certain forms of violence both more feasible and defensible. Put another way, in a political era when state-sanctioned racism is prohibited by law and de facto (if not de jure) racial equality prevails, the racial ambiguity of Latinx populations in relation to whiteness offers nativists the opportunity to deploy racist and dehumanizing accounts of nonwhite "illegals" within a sanctioned legal discourse defined in terms of criminality, sovereignty, legality, and fairness. In sum, opposition to immigration from Mexico and Latin America is the rare issue that combines the pleasures of violent white domination (Herrenvolk practices) with color-blind assertions of the rule of law.

Understanding the politics of Western expansion—especially the participatory politics of Indigenous dispossession and the

56. For more on the complex story regarding Latinos and their relationship to whiteness, see Benjamin Márquez, *LULAC: The Evolution of a Mexican American Political Organization* (Austin: University of Texas Press, 2014); Patrick Lukens, *A Quiet Victory for Latino Rights: FDR and the Controversy over Whiteness* (Tucson: University of Arizona Press, 2012); and Ian Haney López, *White by Law: The Legal Construction of Race* (1996; repr., New York: New York University Press, 2006). A growing number of Latino studies scholars are exploring how Latinos have sometimes claimed whiteness, negotiating not only the Black–white binary but also how they inhabit categories such as not-Black and off-white. Of course, Latinos may recognize themselves as white while also arguing for anti-racist, pro-immigrant policies. But other white-identified Latinos might display their own anti-migrant narratives. Latino police officers, ICE agents—all may (though not necessarily) have a close relationship to whiteness. Some may even fall prey to white supremacy. In sum, whiteness is a vexed category, even for the Latinos who both claim and repudiate it. See Gabriela Resto-Montero, "With the Rise of the Alt-Right, Latino White Supremacy May Not Be a Contradiction in Terms," *Mic*, December 27, 2017.

Mexican-American War—means exploring the relationship between contemporary border politics, anti-migrant sentiment, and an American conception of frontier freedom founded on conquest and the right to movement and expansion. Exploring the conjoined histories of the frontier and the border allows us to see how this racialized legacy of movement and legal and extrajudicial violence have shaped American conceptions of freedom, sovereignty, democracy, citizenship, and the law.[57] In analyzing the politics of Western expansion, I see the Herrenvolk politics of the frontier and the U.S.–Mexican border as representing par-

57. In claiming that a significant portion of conservatives exhibit intense affective reactions against Latinx citizens and noncitizens, I am not arguing that Latinos are the *only* population facing visceral political, racial, and cultural hostility from the Right. Anti-Muslim hysteria is clearly producing particular forms of racialized hate speech and violent xenophobia—as seen in the ongoing efforts of the Trump administration to ban individuals from a variety of countries in Africa and the Middle East. We've seen an increase in anti-Semitic incidents; anti-Asian sentiments are increasingly visible (ranging from long-standing anti-Asian hostility aimed at China and Japan to the racism against South Asians that often merges into Islamophobia to the rise in assaults, harassments, and hate crimes related to the COVID-19 pandemic). Transphobic and misogynist policies attacking the rights of women and sexual minorities have been frequent and ongoing. And of course, anti-Blackness and settler colonialism represent two of the most foundational and dominant racial logics circulating both historically and today. In placing Mexicans at the center of my analysis, I am not calling on political theorists to replace the Black–white binary with a new racial hierarchy that erases or sidelines the significance of other populations and histories. Instead, this essay is a call for developing deeper and more specific knowledge of the various populations that make up the American racial order. In this instance, rather than the all-too-common references to the racial subordination of "Black and Brown people," scholars should move beyond such cursory generalizations and instead provide deeper analyses of the *specific* historical and political dynamics occurring within various racialized populations. See Andrea Smith, "Heteropatriarchy and the Three Pillars of White Supremacy: Rethinking Women of Color Organizing," in *Color of Violence: The INCITE! Anthology*, ed. INCITE! Women of Color against Violence, 66–73 (Boston: South End Press, 2006); see also Bebout, *Whiteness on the Border*, 11.

ticularly rich sites for considering how the movement of certain subjects is understood to be a manifestation of liberty, while the movement of others is deemed unruly, excessive, and dangerous.[58] More specifically, movement on the frontier offered white citizens the freedom to claim territory, challenge borders, and engage in Herrenvolk practices of removal, settlement, and displacement while also acquiring wealth and participating in acts of political creation through founding communities, drawing boundaries, and regulating the movement of others.

Moving between frontier freedom and frontier justice, settlers struggled to establish and extend white democracy, a process involving violent assaults on Mexicans and Indians. By "demonstrating [their] mastery over the unmastered wild," settlers saw themselves as engaged in a violent and epic struggle for the future, willing to risk their lives to bring justice and civilization to a dangerous and savage world.[59]

Today, with Herrenvolk democracy and other forms of white supremacy increasingly socially and legally censured, citizens invested in the politics of nativism and white nationalism remain nostalgically attached to forms of freedom and movement they find increasingly difficult to access. The frontier promise of "perennial rebirth" through practices of violent movement is far less available to white citizens today.[60] No longer animated by a sense of possibility, white nativists today often feel trapped by history, defined by their perceived losses and facing what they see as an increasingly bleak and constricted future. A people who used to think they were captains of the future are now prisoners of the

58. For more on how liberal freedom pivots around the question of movement, see Hagar Kotef, *Movement and the Ordering of Freedom: On Liberal Governance of Mobility* (Durham, N.C.: Duke University Press, 2015).

59. Alexander Livingston, *Damn Great Empires! William James and the Politics of Pragmatism* (New York: Oxford University Press, 2016), 81.

60. Frederick Jackson Turner, "The Significance of the Frontier in American History," 1893, in *Rereading Frederick Jackson Turner . . . and Other Essays* (New Haven, Conn.: Yale University Press, 1998), 2.

past. Defined by a growing sense of injury, white nativists' insistence on their own racial and cultural superiority now coexists alongside popular accounts of demographic, economic, and cultural decline—including a surge in "deaths of despair" among white Americans.[61]

Yet, while nativists are feeling increasingly pessimistic about their own sense of freedom, movement, and futurity, today it is migrants, particularly *unauthorized* migrants, who are on the move, changing their futures, challenging borders, and claiming the right to movement. Prepared to both use and exceed the law in their efforts to achieve freedom and escape repression and subjugation, unauthorized migrants risk their lives to claim opportunity for themselves and their families. Fighting resolutely for new futures in which they can prosper and thrive, migrants are now the population widely perceived as claiming freedom through movement, agents engaged in an epic struggle to both survive and prosper.

Not surprisingly, nativists find this situation infuriating. Historically, the right to move with impunity—to defy, disregard, and reconceive borders—*that* was the purview of white citizenship and frontier freedom. Today, to witness nonwhite migrants claiming their own freedom through movement—and for such action to be seen by many as courageous and worthy of sympathy—provokes intense nativist outrage. Indeed, nativists see such actions as a brutal assault on their own futures. Unable to envision practices of movement outside their own Herrenvolk desires, nativists can only imagine cross-border movement as a form of dispossession and violent domination. Limited by the zero-sum logic of white nationalism, in which migrant flourishing means citizen suffering,

61. See Anne Case and Angus Deaton, *Mortality and Morbidity in the 21st Century*, Brookings Papers on Economic Activity (Washington, D.C.: Brookings Institution Press, 2017), 397–443; Jonathan M. Metzl, *Dying of Whiteness: How the Politics of Racial Resentment Is Killing America's Heartland* (New York: Basic Books, 2019); Annie McClanahan, "Life Expectancies: Mortality, Exhaustion, and Economic Stagnation," *Theory and Event* 22, no. 2 (2019): 360–81.

and compassion for migrants implies a callous disregard for citizens, for nativists in the thrall of whiteness, migrant movement is imagined as an inversion of white democracy—a world where whites are the victims of violence and dispossession as nonwhite populations inflict a vengeful politics of white extinction, open borders, invasion, and racial conquest *(Reconquista)*. Fearful of "losing their country" and being robbed of their history and heritage, revisiting Herrenvolk practices offers nativists a powerful kind of satisfaction and solace.

Today, the desire to experience and revisit Herrenvolk membership is visible in contemporary nativists' rhetoric, associations, actions, and anti-Latinx policies. The outrageous and aggressive speech acts that occur at Trump rallies; the abusive behavior and ugly rhetoric of current and former Border Patrol agents; the paramilitary voluntary border squads; the increasingly violent policies of raids, detentions, and deportations—all of these practices allow nativists to revisit and reenact an available version of settler-colonial and anti-Mexican Herrenvolk politics. For nativists, then, appeals to the "rule of law" are not about equality under the law, an independent judiciary, access to the courts, or abiding by the Constitution; rather, such appeals are about revisiting an era that once sanctioned judicial and extrajudicial violence along racial lines.

The rage of anti-immigrant nativists demonstrates just how profoundly white supremacy has damaged and distorted America's democratic imaginary. Rather than envisioning a multiracial democracy where forms of self-rule are characterized by plenitude, fairness, community, meaningful work, solidarity, joy, movement, and dignity—a vision worth fighting to create together—Herrenvolk logics envision democratic citizenship, freedom, prosperity, and popular sovereignty through racialized narratives of deprivation, exclusion, suffering, and removal. Rather than working to conceive and create a better and more beautiful world, white democracy can think only in terms of a recursive scarcity logic that premises one's own thriving on the denial of such thriving to others. Today, Herrenvolk democracy must be destroyed, and its destruction requires transformative policies as well as an aesthetics of justice that can attract and inspire new multiracial democratic majorities, both in the United States and globally.

1. Freedom on the Frontier: White Democracy and America's Revolutionary Spirit

The Evolution of Whiteness: The Case of Colonial Virginia

In analyzing American history, it's important to recognize that the political meaning of whiteness developed both historically and regionally, emerging through a series of choices that could have gone differently. Acts of dispossession, slavery, and white supremacy were by no means inevitable—they reflect practices, perspectives, and decisions that shaped settler relationships to land and labor, as well as creating particular forms of collective identity and shared governance. To trace this genealogy of whiteness, I want to turn briefly to the history of colonial Virginia. Examining the history of England's first and most important continental colony highlights the unstable condition of whiteness, particularly in the context of racial capitalism. The story of colonial Virginia suggests how the establishment of Herrenvolk republicanism subverted cross-racial political communities and cultivated notions of white freedom.

In *White over Black,* historian Winthrop Jordan observes that in Virginia, the cultivation and export of tobacco produced a desire for labor that was "cheap but not temporary, mobile but not independent."[1] Initially, the colony solved this labor problem through the use of indentured servants.[2] Subject to beatings, abuse, and

1. Winthrop Jordan, *White over Black: American Attitudes toward the Negro, 1550–1812* (1968; repr., Chapel Hill: University of North Carolina Press, 2012), 72.

2. Indentured servants were generally Englishmen bound by contrac-

overwork, a servant might find himself sold without his own consent from one master to another up to the expiration of the indenture. Many did not survive the terms of servitude.[3] However, those who survived and gained their freedom could then work to become planters in their own right. Initially, high mortality rates meant that those who survived their servitude were too few in number to offer serious competition to their former masters. But as the death rate declined and ex-servants continued to make tobacco, freedmen began competing with their former masters.[4]

Bringing with them negative attitudes toward the poor and laboring classes that were common in England, Virginia's masters worried that the increasing number of freedmen would be either dangerously idle or rebellious. In England, the nonpoor had come to view the poor "almost as an alien race, with inbred traits of character that justified plans for their enslavement or incarceration in workhouses."[5] In *American Slavery—American Freedom,* his seminal work on colonial Virginia, Edmund Morgan remarks that such beliefs regarding the poor were "not easy to distinguish from the kind of contempt that today we call racism."[6]

This dynamic of viewing the poor as akin to an "alien race" is what political theorist Cedric Robinson describes in *Black Marxism* as racialism. Insinuating itself into medieval, feudal, and capitalist social structures, racialism marks the tendency of European civilization "not to homogenize but to differentiate—to exaggerate regional, subcultural, and dialectical differences into

---

tual arrangements to serve a master for a specific number of years, usually four to seven, as repayment for their ocean passage, following which the servant would become free.

3. See Edmund Morgan, *American Slavery—American Freedom: The Ordeal of Colonial Virginia* (New York: W. W. Norton, 1975), 129, and Jordan, *White over Black,* 47–48.

4. Morgan, *American Slavery,* 215.

5. Morgan, 385.

6. Morgan, 325.

'racial' ones."[7] The poor were *racial* subjects *within Europe, victims* of dispossession, enclosure, and bondage. Indeed, Robinson suggests that "intra-European racism" was very much a *colonial* process involving invasion, settlement, expropriation, and racial hierarchies.[8] And while Robinson rightly faults Morgan and other historians for paying insufficient attention to these dynamics of European race making, many of their insights nevertheless confirm Robinson's critique. Discussing the violence that early English explorers visited on Indigenous populations, Morgan notes that the treatment of Indigenous peoples in Virginia was "akin to the way Englishmen had behaved in another land" where the natives proved unfriendly:

> The wild Irish had no poisoned arrows and could not put up an effective resistance against invaders. . . . But the Irish . . . were clearly the wrong kind of people. In the English view they were barbarous, only nominally Christian, and generally intractable. . . . The Irish could become good, that is, civil and Christian, only by submission. Those who chose not to submit could be exterminated and replaced by more deserving settlers from England. Sir Humphrey Gilbert, who won his knighthood by subduing the Irish, himself proposed a colony that would bring peace and prosperity to Ireland by replacing rebellious Irish with Englishmen. Later, Gilbert moved from Ireland to the New World.[9]

The contempt and stereotypes aimed at the Irish speak to how the "domination of some Europeans by other Europeans" was seen as both inevitable and natural.[10] Robinson's analysis highlights how racial capitalism evolved from this older order, manifested in a modern world system enmeshed in slavery, violence, imperialism, and genocide. At the same time, the experience of the first

7. Cedric J. Robinson, *Black Marxism: The Making of the Black Radical Tradition* (1983; repr., Chapel Hill: University of North Carolina Press, 2000), 26.

8. Robinson, 67.

9. Morgan, *American Slavery,* 20.

10. Robinson, *Black Marxism,* 26–27.

Africans to arrive in Jamestown in 1619 is a reminder that practices of differentiation are both dynamic and contingent.[11]

As Jordan demonstrates, while negative perceptions of Africans predated English settlement, the social status of Blacks in Virginia was not initially characterized by rightlessness. In the 1630s and 1640s, while some Negroes were serving for life in a hereditary form of slavery, "other Negroes were being released from service like other indentured servants. . . . After the mid-1640s the court records show that other Negroes were incontestably free and were accumulating property of their own."[12] Historical archives show that the first African immigrants—slave, servant, or free—possessed many of the same rights and duties of other Virginians, able to "buy and sell cattle, sue and be sued, earn money, do penance in the church, and if enslaved sometimes purchase their children's freedom, or even their own. Free African Americans held minor political offices, voted, and owned property—including slaves and servants."[13] In sum, Blacks, regardless of class status, initially enjoyed rights that were later denied all Negroes in Virginia.

Even more significantly, the archives of colonial Virginia offer signs that servants and slaves initially felt a sense of identification with one another. And while indentureship was never as dehumanizing as lifetime, hereditary slavery, in their shared exposure to servitude, at least some servants and slaves saw each other as facing a similar predicament. Moreover, as Morgan observes, Virginia "developed her plantation system without slaves,

11. Portuguese ships began supplying the Spanish and Portuguese settlements in America with Negro slaves. By 1550, European enslavement of Blacks was more than a century old, and slavery had become a fixture of the New World. The first Africans arrived in Jamestown, Virginia, in 1619, but as historian Winthrop Jordan has observed, little is known about their precise status during the next twenty years. Slaves formed only a small part of the Virginia labor force until the 1680s. See Jordan, *White over Black,* 44.

12. Jordan, 74.

13. Olson, *Abolition of White Democracy,* 34. Also see Morgan, *American Slavery,* 155.

and slavery introduced no novelties to methods of production. . . . The seventeenth-century plantation already had its separate quartering house or houses for the servants. Their labor was already supervised in groups of eight or ten by an overseer. They were already subject to 'correction' by the whip. They were already underfed and underclothed."[14] In their shared experience laboring on the plantation, Black and white servants bound to the same master "worked, ate, and slept together" and shared in "escapades, escapes, and punishments."[15] It was not uncommon for servants and slaves "to run away together, steal hogs together, get drunk together."[16] Indeed, during Bacon's Rebellion in 1676, "one of the last groups to surrender was a racially mixed band of eighty Negroes and twenty English servants."[17]

Bacon's Rebellion revealed the possibilities of an alliance between white and Black servants and slaves against the policies of the ruling class. However, the rebellion also began as an anti-Indian crusade—a lower-class revolt of discontented, landless men angry at Virginia's colonial governor for denying them permission to retaliate against Native American attacks on settlements and claim additional Indigenous frontier land westward. The rebellion revealed the possibilities of the white and Black poor identifying with each other and uniting in a shared cause. At the same time, the rebellion highlighted how race hatred (in this case, against Indigenous populations) could unite subjects across their differences. For the colony's elite, the lesson of the rebellion was that "resentment of an alien race might be more powerful than resentment of an upper class."[18]

The gradual substitution of African and Indian slavery for white servants after 1680 helped resolve Virginia's labor problems, en-

14. Morgan, *American Slavery,* 308.
15. Morgan, 155.
16. Morgan, 155, 327.
17. Morgan, 327.
18. Morgan, 269–70.

hancing the experience of freedom and equality among whites through the increased degradation of Blacks. For example, in 1705, the Virginia assembly passed an act that "specifically protected the property of servants while confiscating what belonged to slaves" so that "even the small property previously allowed to slaves . . . was to be handed over to poor whites."[19] Laws were passed prohibiting Blacks, regardless of status, from owning firearms. Laws were passed making it illegal for whites to be employed by Blacks. In Virginia, poll taxes were drastically reduced, making it easier for free white men to vote, while free Blacks were being stripped of the right to vote, testify in court, or serve on juries.[20] Over time, Virginia's small farmers began to perceive a common identity with the large, because "neither was a slave. And both were equal in not being slaves."[21] Consequently, struggling farmers began to see their rich neighbors "not as extortionists but as a powerful protector of their common interests." In sum, Virginia "solved the problem" of the poor by enslaving them. Racism became an "essential if unacknowledged" aspect of America's attachment to the values of equality and republicanism.[22]

Settler Freedom: Movement, Removal, Creation, and Participatory Violence

In *The End of the Myth,* historian Greg Grandin states that "all nations have borders, and many today even have walls. But only the United States has had a frontier, or at least a frontier that has served as a proxy for liberation, synonymous with the possibilities and promises of modern life itself."[23] As scholars of settler colo-

19. Morgan, 332–33.
20. See Morgan, 345, and Olson, *Abolition of White Democracy,* 37.
21. Morgan, *American Slavery,* 381.
22. Morgan, 386.
23. Greg Grandin, *The End of the Myth: From the Frontier to the Border Wall in the Mind of America* (New York: Metropolitan, 2019), 3.

nialism and the American frontier have long noted, original conceptions of American identity were based on expansion: "From Jefferson's Presidency to the Mexican War," writes political theorist Michael Rogin, "expansion across the continent was the central fact of American politics."[24] Moreover, as the settlement line moved west, "expansion came to be identified not just as a condition of freedom but as freedom itself."[25] The United States "was a nation founded on the right of freedom, a right not just exercised *by* but originating *in* movement."[26] As Hagar Kotef observes, "free movement was a quintessential element of liberal political thought, with some forms of movement encouraged while other were limited and regulated."[27] This sense of freedom gave settlers a "unique prerogative"—the ability to organize their politics around "the promise of constant, endless expansion."[28] As political philosopher Antonio Negri declares, America's constitutional founding was based on the concept that "space is the expression of freedom." It is the "expansion of space that becomes the horizon of constituent power"—freedom is conceived as "frontier," as the place "where citizens' strength becomes power."[29] As early as 1774, Thomas Jefferson asserted in "A Summary View of the Rights of British America" that "the ability to migrate wasn't just an exercise of natural rights but the source of rights. . . . Liberty was made possible by the right to colonize, letting freemen, when their freedom was threatened, to move on to find free land and carry the torch from one place to another."[30] As Grandin notes, Jefferson provided settlers "a historical and moral philosophy, telling them

24. Michael Paul Rogin, *Fathers and Children: Andrew Jackson and the Subjugation of the American Indian* (New York: Knopf, 1975), 3.

25. Grandin, *End of the Myth,* 42.

26. Grandin, 49.

27. Kotef, "Violent Attachments," 64, 138.

28. Kotef, 94.

29. Antonio Negri, *Insurgencies: Constituent Power and the Modern State* (Minneapolis: University of Minnesota Press, 2009), 142–43.

30. Grandin, *End of the Myth,* 24.

that their movement west wasn't just a fruit of freedom but the source of freedom." By 1805, Thomas Jefferson "couldn't think of any limit to U.S. expansion."[31] In 1824, James Monroe stated, "There is no object which as a people we can desire which we do not possess or which is not within our reach."[32] Here we can see the tension identified by Kotef as well as Hardt and Negri—a conception of sovereignty as "an open, expansive project operating on unbounded terrain" that exists alongside a "fantasy of closure and enclosure," involving "clearly demarcated territory, sealed within a border, which is a container of the people."[33] Here we see that for certain subjects, movement is a manifestation of liberty that should be maximized. While for others, movement is something that must be tightly managed and regulated.[34]

The British colonies in North America were conceived in expansion.[35] The initial frontier, as nineteenth-century Western historian Frederick Jackson Turner reminds us, "was the Atlantic coast. It was the frontier of Europe."[36] For Turner, one of the most significant things about the American frontier is that "it lies on the hither edge of free land."[37] Implying both territorial space and a racialized settler understanding of "free," in Turner's capacious characterization, the frontier came to suggest many things—"a state of mind, a cultural zone . . . a civilizational struggle, a way of life."[38] For Turner, then, the first act of settlement in the wild also defined the frontier. Long before the nation declared its independence, Americans were imagining it as a place of "endless becoming and ceaseless unfurling."[39] As

31. Grandin, 27.
32. James Monroe, State of the Union Address, December 7, 1824.
33. See Michael Hardt and Antonio Negri, *Empire* (Cambridge, Mass.: Harvard University Press, 2001), 165, and Kotef, "Violent Attachments," 119.
34. Kotef, "Violent Attachments," 100.
35. Grandin, *End of the Myth*, 11.
36. Turner, 3.
37. Turner, 2.
38. Grandin, *End of the Myth*, 116.
39. Grandin, 3.

political theorist Alexander Livingston argues, the frontier played "a mythical role in American self-understanding over the course of its transformation from a colony to a nation-state."[40]

America's visions of freedom reflected a dream of settler freedom, founded on reflection and consent as well as "acts of force and fraud."[41] It was on Indigenous land that American settlers "contracted, squabbled, and reasoned with one another." As scholars of settler colonialism have long noted, territorial dispossession was far from a singular event in the nation's emergence.[42] In *Fathers and Children: Andrew Jackson and the Subjugation of the American Indian,* author Michael Rogin notes that America was continually beginning again on the frontier, killing and removing one tribe after another as it expanded across the continent.[43] Indeed, Indian conquest "made the country uniquely American,"[44] with the Indigenous population being "the first enemies the young country had to conquer."[45] As Winthrop Jordan declared, "confronting the Indian in America was a testing experience, common to all the colonies." To "push back the Indian" was to make "a highway for civilization," proving the worth of one's mission.[46] With white citizens fearful that Indian attacks would "annihilate" their "infant communities," frontier freedom represented an ongoing opportunity for white citizens to engage in practices of invasion,

40. Alexander Livingston, *Damn Great Empires! William James and the Politics of Pragmatism* (New York: Oxford University Press, 2016), 80.

41. Rogin, *Fathers and Children,* 3.

42. Claudio Saunt, *Unworthy Republic: The Dispossession of Native Americans and the Road to Indian Territory* (New York: W. W. Norton, 2020); Patrick Wolfe, "Settler Colonialism and the Elimination of the Native," *Journal of Genocide Research* 8, no. 4 (2006): 387–409; Alyosha Goldstein, ed., *Formations of United States Colonialism* (Durham, N.C.: Duke University Press, 2014).

43. Rogin, *Fathers and Children,* 3.

44. Rogin, 7.

45. Rogin, 121.

46. Jordan, *White over Black,* 91.

war, removal, and settlement.[47] In this way, the American desire to claim freedom and resist tyranny was constituted through the imposition of tyranny and unfreedom on others. That America's most powerful and affecting acts of civic creation were simultaneously acts of racialized violence is why it's so difficult for certain white citizens to imagine future acts of creation not characterized by retribution, domination, and loss.

America's revolutionary spirit—what Hannah Arendt refers to as "the principle of public freedom and public happiness"—allowed inhabitants of the colonies to work collectively to establish a republic characterized by "institutions of liberty."[48] To engage in acts of founding was to partake in what Arendt describes as "the human capacity of beginning."[49] During the American Revolution, founders engaged in deliberative practices of "expressing, discussing, and deciding"—participatory acts of political freedom. Yet, beyond the founders, this process of American self-creation and the struggle over the "right to have rights" have always been contingent and contested processes, involving elites as well as those not authorized to make such claims. In the United States, this wide-ranging desire for civic freedom has been enmeshed in a democratic politics shaped by the politics of white supremacy.[50] In the context of western expansion, settlers moving across the frontier continued to win "greater liberty by putting down people of color, and then continuing to define their liberty in opposition to the people of color they put down."[51] Race shaped the bound-

47. Jordan, 120.

48. Hannah Arendt, *On Revolution* (1963; repr., New York: Penguin, 1990), 233–34, 218.

49. Arendt, 223.

50. For more on "dilemma of authorization" and the various practices to which postrevolutionary Americans turned in their desire to seize authority and speak in the people's name, see Jason Frank, *Constituent Moments: Enacting the People in Postrevolutionary America* (Durham, N.C.: Duke University Press, 2010).

51. Grandin, *End of the Myth*, 67.

aries of American membership—creating the economic and social conditions for U.S. assertions and enactments of freedom, democracy, and republican values.[52] And while America's revolutionary spirit can rightly be characterized as the desire for public freedom and public happiness, this desire cannot be decoupled from the fact that what most white Americans came to desire was *white* democracy.[53] During the revolutionary era, white supremacy invited inhabitants of the colonies to be rebels as well as founders, called upon to engage in acts of violence *and* liberation—to destroy and tear down while also "founding anew and building up."

Yet, as Arendt notes, only elected representatives had their participation institutionalized in the Constitution: "The Revolution, while it had given freedom to the people, had failed to provide a space where this freedom could be exercised. Only the representatives of the people, not the people themselves, had an opportunity to engage in those activities of 'expressing, discussing, and deciding' which in a positive sense are the activities of freedom."[54] In contrast to elected representatives, regular citizens were more often than not spectators to the governing of their republic. For the vast majority of citizens, participation in revolutionary politics was through military service rather than deliberative acts of governing. Although only a small minority of citizens regularly engage in practices of public deliberation, the United States has historically offered the people numerous and continual opportu-

52. Lisa Lowe would later develop this critique on an international register, describing the range of connections linking Europe, Africa, Asia, and the Americas through practices of settler colonialism, slavery, and colonial labor relations as "global intimacies"—practices that created the conditions of possibility for Western liberalism. See *Intimacies of Four Continents.*

53. Describing this dynamic, Alexis de Tocqueville characterized America's democracy as an "Anglo-American confederation" where the positions of the two other races ("Indians and the Negroes") were "tangent" to his subject "being American, but not democratic." See Tocqueville, *Democracy in America,* trans. George Lawrence (1835; repr., New York: HarperCollins, 1966), 316.

54. Arendt, *On Revolution,* 235.

nities to participate as citizen-soldiers in wars and conflicts both at home and abroad.[55]

In sum, reckoning with the racialized (and martial) history of American civic life requires acknowledging that the lived *experience* of what most Americans have understood as public freedom and happiness—as collective practices of self-rule—cannot be detached from the political project of whiteness.

White Democracy

As James Baldwin has written (and our earlier discussion of Virginia demonstrated), the act of "becoming white" is a historical as well as moral process that involves the subjugation of Black and other nonwhite populations through practices of settlement and violence.[56] Describing this process, Joel Olson characterizes whiteness as "not a genetic inheritance so much as it is a social relation."[57] To be a "white citizen" is to enjoy the status and privileges of a racial polity, to inhabit "a position of equality and privilege simultaneously: equal to other white citizens yet privileged over those who are not white."[58] Drawing on the work of political theorist Judith Shklar, Olson characterizes whiteness as functioning as a form of social status, what he calls *whiteness as standing*.[59] According to Shklar, the worth of citizenship has historically been less about equality of rights or the political power it imparts than

55. For more on the relationship between war, sexuality, police power, race, and racism in the United States, see Nikhil Pal Singh, *Race and America's Long War* (Berkeley: University of California Press, 2017), and Chandan Reddy, *Freedom with Violence: Race, Sexuality, and the U.S. State* (Durham, N.C.: Duke University Press, 2011).

56. James Baldwin, "On Being White . . . and Other Lies," *Essence Magazine*, April 1984.

57. Olson, *Abolition of White Democracy*, xviii.

58. Olson, xix.

59. Olson, "Whiteness and the Polarization of American Politics," 708.

about conferring dignity and social standing.[60] Acknowledging that this assertion is "not an empirical observation of who had the vote at the time," Olson observes that this is instead a social and affective claim about whiteness as "a *political* color that distinguished the free from the unfree, the equal from the inferior, the citizen from the slave"; citizenship is not just standing, as Shklar argues, but *racialized* standing:[61]

> Whiteness as standing provided a glass floor below which the white citizen could see but never fall. No matter how poor, mean, or ignorant one might have been, or whatever discrimination on the basis of gender, class, religion, or ethnicity one may have been subjected to, one could always derive social esteem (and often draw on public resources) by asserting, "At least I'm not black."[62]

For both Olson and Shklar, "Black people . . . were not simply noncitizens but *anticitizens.*" Not merely excluded from the social compact, African Americans were "the Other that simultaneously threatened and consolidated it."[63] It's my contention that the category *illegal* does similar work. Today, the noncitizen migrant is the Other that both threatens and consolidates white citizenship.

As Du Bois and others have noted, the American racial order has been constituted by an implicit *cross-class alliance* between capital and a section of the white working class. White labor "repressed black labor in the workplace and the community and excluded the latter from full participation in the labor movement."[64] Companies granted white workers higher wages than Blacks and other nonwhites, but more significantly, poor whites (indeed, *all* whites) under slavery, segregation, and Jim Crow and prior to the passage

60. Judith Shklar, *American Citizenship: The Quest for Inclusion* (Cambridge, Mass.: Harvard University Press, 1991), 2.

61. Olson, *Abolition of White Democracy,* 43.

62. Olson, "Whiteness and the Polarization of American Politics," 708. See also Olson, *Abolition of White Democracy,* 43.

63. Olson, *Abolition of White Democracy,* 43.

64. Olson, "Whiteness and the Polarization of American Politics," 707–8.

of civil rights legislation in the 1960s were provided with what historian David Roediger refers to as the "wages of whiteness." Drawing on Du Bois's groundbreaking work *Black Reconstruction,* Roediger characterizes these wages as "public, psychological, and material."[65] Describing this dynamic, Du Bois writes,

> The white group of laborers, while they received a low wage, were compensated in part by a sort of public and psychological wage. They were given public deference and titles of courtesy because they were white. They were admitted freely with all classes of white people to public functions, public parks, and the best schools. The police were drawn from their ranks. . . . Their vote selected public officials, and while this had small effect on their economic situation, it had great effect upon their personal treatment and the deference shown them.[66]

For Du Bois, in addition to the crucial fundamentals of political power, such as being empowered by the state to enforce the law and having the right to vote, the "public and psychological" wages of whiteness were serious and significant, ranging from affective practices (whiteness as a *feeling* that involved practices of courtesy and deference) to forms of access that were public (unlike Blacks, whites had access to *all* public accommodations—parks, public schools, and any other public spaces they sought to inhabit), as well as admission into any neighborhood or establishment they could afford to occupy. As Matthew Frye Jacobson has written (and our earlier discussion has demonstrated), the white citizen is not a static figure that is unchanging across time and space. Instead, laws and *moeurs*—practices of domination, racial performance, and displacement—work together to produce the white citizen.

Supported "through the explicit or tacit consent of local, state, and federal governments," white democracy is "not a guarantee of equality among whites but . . . a form of racial standing. . . . It does not make all whites absolute equals, but that was never the intent

65. Roediger, *Wages of Whiteness,* xx.
66. Du Bois, *Black Reconstruction in America,* 700–701.

of white citizenship. It just ensures that no white ever need find himself or herself at the absolute bottom of the social and political barrel, because that position is already taken."[67] Whiteness served as "a badge of status that indicated full membership in a community and rights to all the accompanying perquisites: the right to vote, to earn, to prosper, to educate one's children, to own a firearm, even to riot."[68] As Edmund Morgan demonstrated, not only did slavery allow small farmers in Virginia to prosper; it also allowed them to acquire "social, psychological, and political advantages" that aligned them with upper-class whites.[69] White elites were often quite explicit about the comparative and cross-class pleasures that came with whiteness under slavery. Confederate soldier, southern politician, author, and slaveholder Thomas Reade Rootes Cobb echoed Du Bois's analysis in his claim that "every [white] citizen feels that he belongs to an elevated class. It matters not that he is not slaveholder; he is not of the inferior race; his is a freeborn citizen. . . . The poorest meets the richest as an equal; sits at his table with him; salutes him as a neighbor; meets him in every public assembly; and stands on the same social platform."[70] In this sense, whiteness, as Noel Ignatiev and John Garvey argue, means that the race's "most wretched members share a status higher, in certain respects, than that of the most exalted persons excluded from it."[71] In the era of Herrenvolk democracy, white standing "was akin to aristocratic privilege. Once achieved, it was inheritable, stable, and enduring."[72]

White supremacy and racial domination also served as one of the few participatory practices of American democracy. Slavery

67. Olson, "Whiteness and the Polarization of American Politics," 709, and Olson, *Abolition of White Democracy,* 29–30.

68. Olson, *Abolition of White Democracy,* 44.

69. Morgan, *American Slavery,* 344.

70. T. R. R. Cobb, quoted in Jenkins, *Pro-Slavery Thought in the Old South,* 193; Olson, *Abolition of White Democracy,* 39.

71. Noel Ignatiev and John Garvey, eds., *Race Traitor* (New York: Routledge, 1996), 9–10.

72. Olson, *Abolition of White Democracy,* 74.

and Jim Crow, for example, gave everyday white Americans the right to police and punish African Americans, demanding that nonwhite subjects acquiesce to humiliating codes of racial etiquette and invoking the authority of the law to exert domination over the movement and placement of Black bodies.[73] Describing the active role played by white citizens in the daily creation of segregated space, historian C. Vann Woodward observes that Jim Crow laws "put the authority of the state or city in the voice of the street-car conductor, the railway brakeman, the bus driver, the theater usher, and also into the voice of the hoodlum of the public parks and playgrounds. . . . They gave free rein and the majesty of the law to mass aggressions that might otherwise have been curbed, blunted, or deflected."[74]

Legislated by white elected officials and enforced by a broad cross section of white citizens (waiters/waitresses, realtors, hospital workers, librarians, ushers, lifeguards, landlords, hotel clerks, etc.), Jim Crow gave ordinary white citizens the power, opportunity, and freedom to personally exert authority over the spaces African Americans inhabited and/or sought to inhabit. Every law designed to restrict the freedom of nonwhite peoples (the post–Civil War Black Codes, Jim Crow, etc.) reminds us that Herrenvolk democracy was a mass-based, participatory endeavor, reproduced and administered from both above and below. Indeed, the conjoined histories of racial capitalism and Herrenvolk democracy expose the uncomfortable fact that "neither slavery nor segregation nor

73. Of course, Jim Crow was also sometimes applied to other populations deemed nonwhite, including (at particular times and in particular regions) Mexicans and Puerto Ricans. See Darius Echeverría, "Beyond the Black–White Binary Construction of Race: Mexican Americans, Identity Formation, and the Pursuit of Public Citizenship," *Journal of American Ethnic History* 28, no. 1 (2008): 104–11. However, for populations deemed not-Black, segregation was unevenly applied, while for African Americans, it was a much more consistent and pervasive system.

74. C. Vann Woodward, *The Strange Career of Jim Crow* (New York: Oxford University Press, 1955), 93.

any other form of racial domination could have survived without the tacit or explicit consent of the white majority."[75]

Of course, to think about white democracy is also to consider how whiteness is a gendered phenomenon, enmeshed in questions of embodiment and sexuality. Performances of whiteness and white supremacy have often involved practices of violence, domination, control, and deference related to the control of women's bodies that are deeply patriarchal in nature. Moreover, conceptions of masculinity are always simultaneously gendered and racialized.[76] In the context of white democracy, it's important to remember that white women existed under conditions of serious and significant inequality, positioned as the legal and social dependents of white men. Until the mid-nineteenth century and the passage of Married Women's Property Acts, the practice of *coverture* meant that a married white woman had no legal existence separate from her husband. Married women could not own property in their own name, could not enter into contracts, and often could not control their own earnings;[77] *marital rape* was oxymoronic, since a wife was legally a husband's sexual property.[78]

At the same time, white women, despite their own subjugation,

75. Olson, *Abolition of White Democracy,* xv–xvi.

76. See Michael Kimmel, *Angry White Men: American Masculinity at the End of an Era* (New York: Bold Type, 2017); Aida Hurtado and Mrinal Sinha, *Beyond Machismo: Intersectional Latino Masculinities* (Austin: University of Texas Press, 2016); Kathy Ferguson, *The Man Question: Visions of Subjectivity in Feminist Theory* (Berkeley: University of California Press, 1993); Wendy Brown, *Manhood and Politics: A Feminist Reading in Political Theory* (Lanham, Md.: Rowman and Littlefield, 1988).

77. By contrast, a single white woman could sometimes own property and make contracts in her own name. See Marylynn Salmon, *Women and the Law of Property in Early America* (Chapel Hill: University of North Carolina Press, 1986).

78. Indeed, early rape laws defined sexual assault as a property crime against the husband or father whose wife or daughter had been "defiled." See Kersti Yllö and M. Gabriela Torres, eds., *Marital Rape: Consent, Marriage and Social Change in Global Context* (New York: Oxford University Press, 2016).

helped enforce white supremacist racial hierarchies.[79] As feminist and queer of color critiques have shown, alongside inequality and gender oppression, white women had access to certain rights due to their racial standing. While white married women were dependent and denied a separate legal existence from their husbands, Black female slaves had no rights whatsoever.[80] Black slaves were not legally allowed to marry; they had no rights to their children; their families could be split apart at will.[81] In contrast to the anticitizenship of African American women, white women "were

79. See Olson, *Abolition of White Democracy,* 33, 53–59; Elizabeth Gillespie McRae, *Mothers of Massive Resistance: White Women and the Politics of White Supremacy* (New York: Oxford University Press, 2018); Glenda Elizabeth Gilmore, *Gender and Jim Crow: Women and the Politics of White Supremacy in North Carolina, 1896–1920* (Chapel Hill: University of North Carolina Press, 1996); June Melby Benowitz, *Days of Discontent: American Women and Right-Wing Politics, 1933–1945* (DeKalb: Northern Illinois University Press, 2002); June Melby Benowitz, *Challenge and Change: Right-Wing Women, Grassroots Activism, and the Baby Boom Generation* (Gainesville: University Press of Florida, 2017); Andrea Dworkin, *Right-Wing Women: The Politics of Domesticated Females* (New York: Perigee, 1983).

80. For more on how the practices of white supremacy have shaped the politics of gender and sexuality, see Audre Lorde, *Sister Outsider: Essays and Speeches* (1981; repr., New York: Crossing/Penguin, 2012); Cherríe Moraga and Gloria Anzaldúa, eds., *This Bridge Called My Back: Writings by Radical Women of Color* (1981; repr., Albany: SUNY Press, 2015); Akasha (Gloria T.) Hull, Patricia Bell-Scott, and Barbara Smith, eds., *But Some of Us Are Brave: Black Women Studies* (1982; repr., New York: Feminist Press at CUNY, 2015); Barbara Smith, *Home Girls: A Black Feminist Anthology* (1983; repr., New Brunswick, N.J.: Rutgers University Press, 2000); bell hooks, *Talking Back: Thinking Feminist Thinking Black* (1989; repr., New York: Routledge, 2015); Gloria Anzaldúa, ed., *Making Face, Making Soul/Haciendo Caras: Creative and Critical Perspectives by Feminists of Color* (San Francisco: Aunt Lute, 1990); and Roderick Ferguson, *Aberrations in Black: Toward a Queer of Color Critique* (Minneapolis: University of Minnesota Press, 2013).

81. Hortense Spillers, "Mama's Baby, Papa's Maybe: An American Grammar Book," *Diacritics* 17, no. 2 (1987): 64–81; also see Shatema Threadcraft, *Intimate Justice: The Black Female Body and the Body Politic* (New York: Oxford University Press, 2016).

within the polity but not the public sphere."[82] For Olson, "the distinction between dependent citizenship and anticitizenship" in the context of coverture helps explain the relationship between gender and race in the United States.[83] While white citizenship is certainly patriarchal, white supremacist practices of white democracy were not (and have not been) exclusive to one gender.

Movement and Dispossession/Settler and Lawgiver: From Outlaw to Enforcer

Marking the end of the Revolutionary War, the 1783 signing of the Treaty of Paris set the new nation's western border at the Mississippi River. The treaty's first article recognized the independence of the original thirteen colonies; the second article ceded the territory between the Alleghenies and the Mississippi.[84] Later, under Jefferson's administration, the Louisiana Purchase extended the nation across the Mississippi, nearly doubling the country's size. According to historian Peter Onuf, "President Jefferson's vision of westward expansion projected that glorious struggle into the future and across the continent" as "a kind of permanent revolution, reenacting the nation's beginnings in the multiplication of new, self-governing republican states."[85] As Arendt notes, of the founders, it was Jefferson who expressed the most concern that the Constitution provided a space "only for the representatives of the people, and not for the people themselves."[86] According to Jefferson, it was "'universal law' which 'nature' had 'given to all men' that allowed his 'ancestors' the right to leave their country of birth and go 'in quest of new habitations, and of there establishing new societies.'"[87]

82. Olson, *Abolition of White Democracy,* 59.
83. Olson, 33.
84. Grandin, *End of the Myth,* 24.
85. Peter S. Onuf, *The Mind of Thomas Jefferson* (Charlottesville: University of Virginia Press, 2007), 107.
86. Arendt, *On Revolution,* 238.
87. Grandin, *End of the Myth,* 24.

Offering citizens access to new land, westward expansion transformed the settler into a lawgiver, a subject who both establishes and wields the law. Launching themselves into the frontier, settlers staged, over and over again, this vision of, in Onuf's phrase, permanent revolution. In this vision of freedom, "nature was boundless and . . . the frontier would serve as a place of perennial rebirth."[88] Moreover, because English law concerning succession to property "was abolished in almost all the states at the time of Revolution," the laws of inheritance in the new republic were *not* based on primogeniture, ending the feudal restriction on "the right of the father to dispose of his estate as he wished."[89] With fathers no longer required to leave their estates to their eldest male heirs, American inheritance law called for "the equal sharing of a father's property among his children."[90] With property being divided more equally, this changing relationship to property and wealth—"between family feeling and preservation of the land"—created fresh incentives for white settlers to go west in search of "virgin soil" to claim and create property for themselves.[91] At the same time, to experience the freedom of founding and the pleasures of being a lawgiver was *also* to partake in the politics of whiteness—to be an independent subject authorized to both establish and transcend the law.

Fundamental to Herrenvolk democracy is its paradoxical quality of white citizens ruling themselves democratically while simultaneously imposing tyranny over a nonwhite majority,[92] functioning "through a combination of democratic decision-making by white majorities and extralegal practices of terror," Olson writes. "The white majority not only makes the law but decides whether, how,

88. Grandin, 25.

89. Turner, "Significance of the Frontier," 54; Rogin, *Fathers and Children,* 89.

90. Rogin, *Fathers and Children,* 89; Turner, "Significance of the Frontier," 54, 52.

91. Turner, "Significance of the Frontier," 53.

92. van den Berghe, *Race and Racism,* 101.

and on whom it will be enforced. White tyranny does not contradict the democratic will but is an expression of it."[93]

Under the Herrenvolk system in the United States, white citizens made laws that gave them the legal right to decide "whether, how, and on whom" laws would be enforced while also targeting nonwhite populations who were generally excluded from making the laws by which they were ruled.[94] Moreover, as Mary Young observed, in justifying the dispossession and destruction of native communities, white citizens resolved this moral dilemma by cultivating an image of themselves as virtuous, law-abiding Americans who enter into "free contract" with others. The logics of Herrenvolk democracy offered settlers a racialized framework that allowed them to reconcile "avarice with honor."[95] Indeed, the settler "lust for the land" led white frontiersmen to continually move onto Indian land, violating treaties as soon as they were signed.[96] Describing the "successful but unauthorized expeditions" that destroyed Chickamauga towns in 1794, Michael Rogin observes that frontier expansion involved continually invading Indian boundaries. Whites "signed treaties only to move onto lands retained by Indians and bought and sold land in Indian country." Want "was legitimated in the language of law."[97]

Not only did Herrenvolk democracy give white settlers the chance to "legitimate want"; it also encouraged the tendency move between the legal and the extralegal, to both *wield* the law and *exceed* the law. Scholars of the West describe numerous instances of "frontier barbarism" whereby settlers terrorized, tortured, and murdered Native Americans only to have such deeds not only go unpunished but be rewarded. A classic example is

93. Olson, *Abolition of White Democracy*, 65.

94. The Civil Rights and Restorative Justice Project, "Reading Room," Northeastern University School of Law.

95. Mary Elizabeth Young, *Redskins, Ruffleshirts, and Rednecks: Indian Allotments in Alabama and Mississippi 1830–1860* (Norman: University of Oklahoma Press, 1961), 3.

96. Rogin, *Fathers and Children*, 132.

97. Rogin, 132, 133.

the case of Frederick Stump, an eighteenth-century settler who moved his family onto land beyond the boundaries of settlement. After natives reportedly killed his family, he engaged in a "course of retribution," hunting native people throughout the area. In 1768, Stump and his German servant murdered eleven "friend-Indians," as British officials called the victims—five men, three women, and three children. "They scalped the dead and disposed of the bodies, throwing some in a hole hacked in a frozen river and burning the rest."[98] Yet, following their capture, a mob, "made up of seventy to eighty white vigilantes and said to include members of the still-active Paxton Boys,[99] came to their rescue. Armed with guns and tomahawks, the mob swarmed the old log jail where the two murderers were being held, in the town of Carlisle, and set them free. Neither Stump nor Eisenhauer was ever brought to justice."[100]

Under Herrenvolk democracy, not only could white citizens practice "vigilante justice" by engaging in extrajudicial punishment—for example, lynchings—but self-appointed white citizens could also (as in the Stump incident) choose to *pardon* those they felt had been treated unjustly. Stump eventually fled through Georgia and into Tennessee, where he became a successful whiskey distiller and a slaver.[101] Later, Stump earned the rank of captain in Tennessee's first militia expedition, "clearing Creeks and Choctaws off the road from Nashville to Natchez." A recipient of Herrenvolk justice, Stump "was transformed from an outlaw into an agent of the law."[102]

98. Grandin, *End of the Myth*, 22.

99. The Paxton Boys were a group of Scotch-Irish frontiersmen who "rampaged through western Pennsylvania, murdering scores of Conestoga, scalping their victims and mutilating their corpses." Grandin, 21. Following the Conestoga Massacre, the Paxton Boys formed a vigilante mob to protest the central government and the claim that they weren't doing enough to protect setters. See Grandin, 57–58. The Paxton Boys gained a large number of allies throughout the colony and were never punished for their murder or crimes.

100. Grandin, 22.

101. Grandin.

102. Grandin.

The story of Frederick Stump is an example of how important it is to analyze the practices of Herrenvolk democracy not only in terms of slavery and Jim Crow but in terms of settler colonialism, border violence, and territorial dispossession. The failure to seriously theorize native and Latinx populations in relation to white democracy works to reinscribe a Black–white racial binary that leaves scholars less able to analyze how questions of land and the promise of limitless movement and shifting borders have shaped race politics in the Americas. At the same time, while scholars of the frontier help turn our attention to issues of expansion and movement, their analysis of race can be overly spatial, failing to adequately theorize how white racial standing represents practices of freedom and impunity that are both regionally distinctive and also national and ubiquitous. For example, Grandin argues that the frontier can be understood as a kind of "safety valve" in which the boundlessness and logic of endless growth and expansion played a key role in "deflecting domestic extremism" and "relegating racism and extremism to the fringe" of American life.[103] Describing Frederick Jackson Turner's frontier thesis, Grandin notes that Turner constructed a myth with "the experience of westward expansion overcoming sectional loyalties and racial animosities, leading to a true humanism, nurturing open-minded citizens capable of addressing of mass industrial society with applied, progressive, and responsible policies." Grandin refers to this as Turner's "centrist pioneer progressivism," arguing that Turner's "frontier universalism, along with its imagined suppression of extremism, could only be maintained through ceaseless expansion."[104] Likewise, Alexander Livingston draws on the work of Richard Slotkin to analyze how "the wild" has been figured in the nation's psyche "as a space of moral renewal and regeneration."[105] Moving between empirical depiction and myth, Livingston de-

103. Grandin, 7.
104. Grandin, 131.
105. Livingston, *Damn Great Empires!*, 80–81.

clares that the frontier "symbolizes a mythic state of exception where this ritual of moral and civic regeneration through violence can take place . . . through westward expansion."[106]

Although undeniably insightful, such accounts can lose sight of how the white supremacist logics of Herrenvolk democracy suffused America's racial imaginary far beyond the frontier. To understand expansion as relegating racism and extremism to the "fringe" of American life is to fall prey to what Ian Angus refers to as a kind of "geographic determinism" that equates a particular politics with a particular understanding of place.[107] While the frontier *did* sometimes produce a "horizon of constituent power" and feelings of freedom and equality between white citizens, such experiences were grounded in a vision of expansion and open spaces undergirded by notions of white equality via white racial standing that were visible far beyond the frontier. Indeed, theorizing Herrenvolk democracy helps us see how whiteness *is itself* a practice of space making and space claiming. More than the frontier, it was white supremacy that relieved various political pressures, created opportunities for wildness, and deflected certain forms of domestic extremism from dividing the white polity.

Centering focus less on Turner's mythology and more on the realities of Indian dispossession and Mexican conquest allows us to see how ceaseless expansion is not a safety valve *against* domestic extremism; rather, the expansion authorized by white democracy *is itself* domestic extremism. Moreover, while the frontier did stage particular forms of racial violence and produce particular regional conceptions of American identity, such violence was certainly not relegated to the "fringe" or "edge" of the United States—

106. Livingston, 81.

107. For more on how the tendency to conflate expansion with liberty produces an inability to consider how boundaries and limits can be something other than repressive, see Ian Angus, "Empire, Borders, Place: A Critique of Hardt and Negri's Concept of Empire," *Theory and Event* 7, no. 3 (2004).

it was ongoing and everywhere. And the frontier may have served as a "mythic state of exception," but this state of exception was never confined to the frontier. *White supremacy is the state of exception.* From slave patrols to draft riots, white Americans claimed the freedom to partake in extralegal forms of racial terrorism in cities and towns across the nation.[108] Engaging in rituals of moral and civic regeneration through violence, and able to transcend the rule of law in the name of a racialized public good, Herrenvolk democracy gave white citizens the freedom to decide who or what lies inside or outside the structure of law.

Reporting on mob violence in New Orleans, Ida B. Wells-Barnett looked to capture the wild freedom and impunity that white rioters felt in engaging in violent assaults and disobeying the various calls to maintain order.[109] Writing on the practices of lynching and mob violence, Wells-Barnett stressed how white democracy gave ordinary Americans the opportunity to break the law with impunity. Du Bois aptly characterizes this era of mob violence as "a sort of permissible Roman holiday for the entertainment of vicious whites."[110] Pointing to the fact that in the span of four days, more than a thousand African Americans in New Orleans were injured and fifteen were killed, Wells-Barnett writes,

> During the entire time the mob held the city in its hands and went about holding up street cars and searching them, taking from them colored men to assault, shoot, and kin, chasing colored men upon the public square . . . breaking into the homes of defenseless colored men and women and beating aged and decrepit men and women to death, the police and the legally-constituted authorities showed plainly where their sympathies were, for in no case reported through the daily papers does there appear the arrest, trial and conviction of one

108. See Iver Bernstein, *The New York City Draft Riots: Their Significance for American Society and Politics in the Age of the Civil War* (New York: Oxford University Press, 1990), and Sally E. Hadden, *Slave Patrols: Law and Violence in Virginia and the Carolinas* (Cambridge, Mass.: Harvard University Press, 2003).

109. Wells-Barnett, *Mob Rule in New Orleans,* 230.

110. Du Bois, *Black Reconstruction in America,* 701.

> of the mob for any of the brutalities which occurred. The ringleaders of the mob were at no time disguised. . . . The murderers still walk the streets of New Orleans, well known and absolutely exempt from prosecution.[111]

In thinking about this legacy of racialized terror, Olson reminds us that although white mob violence is often represented as "a sad aberration of democracy," the white citizens who gathered in the streets often "took themselves to be protectors of republican institutions." Creating racialized rituals of moral and civic regeneration through violence, mob leaders in New Orleans, Philadelphia, and New York "presented themselves as patriots. . . . Mobs christened themselves with names like the Sons of Liberty and the Minutemen. The mobs saw anti-Black riots as absolutely democratic, whether they involved tarring Black people or smashing abolitionist presses."[112] Lynch mobs were yet another democratic form of mass action in which white citizens were able to both break and wield the law, asserting their ability as a sovereign people to transcend the rule of law in the name of justice and the public good. Indeed, as historian Amy Wood has demonstrated, for whites who supported and participated in lynchings and other acts of extralegal violence, "issues of racial order went beyond the law, infractions against the order were subject to a greater justice." Woods notes that during the 1893 lynching of Henry Smith, the mob in Paris, Texas, scrawled the word "JUSTICE" on the platform where Smith was burned and tortured.[113]

Beyond acts of spectacular violence, the ability to regard oneself as law abiding while being free to engage in violent and despotic behavior toward nonwhite subjects reflects a fundamental element of Herrenvolk democracy. Describing this dynamic,

111. Wells-Barnett, *Mob Rule in New Orleans,* 244–45.

112. Olson, *Abolition of White Democracy,* 32.

113. Amy Louise Wood, *Lynching and Spectacle: Witnessing Racial Violence in America, 1890–1940* (Chapel Hill: University of North Carolina Press, 2009), 43.

Du Bois quotes the German American reformer Carl Schurz, who observed,

> Wherever I go—the street, the shop, the house, the hotel, or the steamboat—I hear the people talk in such a way as to indicate that they are yet unable to conceive of the Negro as possessing any rights at all. Men who are honorable in their dealings with their white neighbors, will cheat a Negro without feeling a single twinge of their honor. To kill a Negro they do not deem murder; to debauch a Negro woman, they do not think fornication; to take the property away from a Negro they do not consider robbery.[114]

In Schurz's depiction of white citizens "unable to conceive" that a Negro could possess "any rights at all," we hear echoes of Supreme Court chief justice Roger B. Taney's assertion in the *Dred Scott* decision that African Americans "had no rights which the white man was bound to respect."[115] White supremacy gave white Americans license to become un-self-consciously criminal—to cheat, assault, and steal while maintaining one's sense of law abidingness, decency, and virtue.

In thinking about the practice of Herrenvolk democracy, it's important to recognize how multilayered the phenomenon is when it comes to the practice of white participation. For while *all* white citizens receive the benefits of white democracy, only *some* white citizens chose to engage in *embodied* acts of extrajudicial violence (doing the raping or killing, performing the lynching, joining the mob, beating the nonwhite person). Other forms of participation were also immoral but often indirect: *attending* the lynching, cheering on the mob, choosing to not contact the police, serving on the all-white jury, refusing to convict, wearing/watching blackface, using racial slurs, enforcing Jim Crow, refusing to hire or rent to or serve nonwhites. This wide array of actions and practices highlights how profoundly *participatory* white democracy has been.

114. Du Bois, *Black Reconstruction in America,* 136.

115. Library of Congress, *The "Dred Scott" Decision: Opinion of Chief Justice Taney* (Washington, D.C., [1857] 1860).

Moreover, white supremacy's very diversity produces powerful forms of denial and disassociation. Under Herrenvolk democracy, not only did white citizens have the freedom to engage in legal and extrajudicial acts of tyranny against nonwhite subjects—the decision *not* to engage in the most bloody and overt forms of brutality sometimes worked to obscure other forms of white democracy and other forms of white complicity. Overt acts of violence could be denied and denounced—whites could focus on the violence and express opposition to and disgust with such "excesses." But alongside such statements and generalized opposition, from the seventeenth to the mid-twentieth centuries, only a minority of white citizens organized to put a stop to white mob violence, with such violence generally going unpunished.

Jacksonian Democracy and Settler Sovereignty

The deep association between white democracy, territorial dispossession, and the American experience of equality and freedom was deepened and reinforced under the presidency of Andrew Jackson. A man whose early career involved personally driving a slave coffle as well as providing legal assistance to and processing the claims of whites who'd taken land from Native Americans, Jackson's very identity was steeped in a larger folklore that highlighted a history of violence against nonwhites.[116] Stories of

116. Given his racial politics, we should not be surprised that Donald Trump often cites Andrew Jackson as his favorite American president and the one with whom he feels the most affinity. After touring Jackson's plantation in 2017, Trump stated, "Inspirational visit, I have to tell you. I'm a fan." Trump had a portrait of the seventh president hung next to his desk in the Oval Office at the start of his term in 2016. See "Trump Cites Andrew Jackson as His Hero—and a Reflection of Himself," *Washington Post*, March 15, 2017. On June 26, Trump signed an executive order to prosecute anyone attempting to destroy or vandalize a monument, memorial, or statue, signing the order following attempts by protesters to pull down the statue of Andrew Jackson in Washington, D.C.'s, Lafayette Square. Trump has called the Jackson statue "a great monument."

Jackson keeping "the skulls of Indians he killed as trophies, and his soldiers cut long strips of skin from their victims to use as bridle reins," have long been part of his legend.[117] Yet seen through the logics of Herrenvolk democracy, we can see that for Jackson, to be a white freeman involved not only the right to self-preservation but a natural "right to violence."[118] In a revealing account from this period, it was said that Jackson "flew into a rage" when a federal agent asked for Jackson's passport while he was moving a slave coffle along the Natchez Trace and passing through Chickasaw and Choctaw lands (at the time, whites were required to carry proof they owned the slaves traveling with them through Indian country).[119] Unwilling to show his papers, Jackson found the agent's request to be "an insulting assault on his rights," worked to get him fired, and threatened him with vigilante justice.[120] As Grandin observes, Jackson's definition of sovereign liberty "imagined 'freeborn' to mean white born and 'liberty' to mean the ability to do whatever they wanted, including to buy and sell humans and move them, unrestrained by interior frontiers, across a road that by treaty belonged to an indigenous nation. To be asked for a passport was akin to slavery itself, and to be so asked in front of actual enslaved people signaled 'that their owners were not the sovereigns after all.'"[121]

This reaction to being asked to "show papers" is indicative of Jackson's belief that white freedom meant freedom from restraint, including "from authorities telling them they couldn't be slaver or

117. Grandin, *End of the Myth,* 51. In a coffle, slaves would have a U-shaped piece of metal, or yoke, put around their necks. The yoke was attached to a long pole, with the pole containing a number of yokes, each holding one slave, so that the group of slaves were chained together in a line.

118. Grandin, 54; Rogin, *Fathers and Children,* 42.

119. Grandin, *End of the Myth,* 51; Rogin, *Fathers and Children,* 41.

120. Grandin, *End of the Myth,* 51.

121. Grandin, 52.

settler."[122] In the Jacksonian era, enhanced democracy and racial exclusion were conjoined through "universal manhood suffrage." Yet the extension of white male suffrage often led directly to the disenfranchisement of free Black men (and some white women) who had voted since the colonial period. Justifying removal in the name of settler sovereignty, Jackson signed the Indian Removal Act into law in 1830. Federal troops were instructed to push Native Americans beyond the Mississippi, extinguishing their titles to their land. The first removal resulted in about 25 million acres of formerly Indian land, including large tracts of Georgia and Alabama, to be freed up for the market and slave economy.[123]

Thus, in the face of multiple forms of racial domination—slavery growing in the South, Native Americans being driven west—"white settlers and planters who got their land experienced something equally unprecedented: an extraordinary degree of power and popular sovereignty. Never before in history could so many white men consider themselves so free."[124] Jacksonian democracy gave white citizens enhanced access to a variety of democratic and civil rights alongside newfound forms of economic opportunity—increased access to property; expansion of the franchise, freedom of speech, association, and assembly; the right to bear arms; a free press; the right to a jury of one's peers. Under Jacksonian democracy, equality and opportunity were simultaneously *more* racialized *and* more widely distributed. As Olson writes, "equality and liberty went from abstract principles to lived experiences for the masses of ordinary men . . . not as universally held rights but as privileges reserved for members of the white club. White citizenship represents the democratization of social status, extending it from the upper class to the masses by transforming it from a perk of wealth to a perk of race."[125]

122. Grandin, 58.
123. Grandin, 59.
124. Grandin, 67.
125. Olson, *Abolition of White Democracy,* 44.

Until Lincoln's election in 1860, Jackson's successors "continued to unite slavers and settlers" under a banner of freedom defined as "freedom from restraint . . . on slaving, freedom from restraints on dispossessing, freedom from restraints on moving west."[126] Seeking to align their beliefs with their desires, Jacksonian settlers sought to "remove Indians, wage war on Mexico, and defend and extend slavery."[127] Founded on conquest and the right to movement and expansion, policies such as the Indian Removal Act serve as a reminder that these same conceptions of settler sovereignty also assured white citizens that nonwhite populations could be removed and relocated. In other words, the corollary to freedom as movement was freedom as removal.

126. Grandin, *End of the Myth*, 96.
127. Grandin, 56.

2. A Desire for Land but Not People: *Herrenvolk* Democracy and the Violent Legacies of the Mexican-American War

> The province of Texas is still part of the Mexican dominions, but it will soon contain no Mexicans; the same thing has occurred whenever the Anglo-Americans have come into contact with populations of a different origin.
>
> —ALEXIS DE TOCQUEVILLE, *Democracy in America*

IN HIS DISCUSSION of the "laws and mores" of the United States, Alexis de Tocqueville was frank in acknowledging the racialized parameters of Jacksonian democracy. Describing the United States as an "Anglo-American confederation," Tocqueville characterized Black and Indigenous people as "tangents to my subjects, being American, but not democratic."[1] Yet despite his assertion in the first volume that these "three races" defined the American project, by the time he was writing the second volume, Tocqueville was already acknowledging that other nonwhite populations beyond "Indians and Negroes" were part of the United States. One of these groups was Mexicans. Interestingly—as the epigraph to this chapter shows—in prognosticating about this "new" population, Tocqueville's account simultaneously recognizes and disappears them. This practice of acknowledgment and erasure would

1. Grandin, 316.

become a familiar part of the Anglo racial imaginary—particularly when addressing the Mexican presence in the United States.

As the frontier pushed ever farther west, American settlers were increasingly encountering Mexicans—citizens of a neighboring sovereign nation and a new racialized population to be feared, exploited, and subjugated. "Native Americans and African Americans had long been used to mark the line between freedom and abandon," Greg Grandin writes. "Now Mexicans helped secure that psychic border."[2]

The Mexican-American War (1846–48) is often overlooked as a formative conflict in American history, perhaps unsurprisingly considering that the Civil War began only thirteen years later. But it's key to understanding how the legacy of white democracy has come to shape contemporary border politics. Historian Steven Hahn has described the war as emboldening "some of the most aggressive political and cultural tendencies in American life," helping to establish a particular image of frontier freedom founded on conquest and the right to land, movement, and expansion.[3] Indeed, in 1836, when Texas won its independence from Mexico, President Jackson stated that annexing the Republic of Texas would expand America's "area of freedom" and extend its "circle of free institutions."[4] However, the conception of freedom being articulated by the Anglo[5] settlers of the Texas republic was

2. Grandin, 92.

3. Steven Hahn, *A Nation without Borders: The United States and Its World in an Age of Civil Wars, 1830–1910* (New York: Penguin, 2016), 132.

4. Grandin, *End of the Myth*, 84.

5. In this section, I often use the term *Anglo* when talking about white settlers. In doing this, I'm drawing on the work of Latinx studies scholars who study racial politics in the American Southwest. In his note on terminology, Arnoldo de Leon defines *Anglos* as "any white, English-speaking, non-Mexican American." As Mark Allan Goldberg notes, while the term *Anglo* is closely associated with *Anglo-Saxon*, in the Southwest, the term did not simply refer to people of English descent. Instead, since the late eighteenth century, the term *Anglo* was used to distinguish U.S.-born whites from American Indians and from ethnic Mexicans. And while whiteness is

deeply racialized: not only were most settlers originally from the Deep South but many were "land speculators, slavers, militia leaders, and Indian killers."[6]

Such racialized politics had a profound impact on class conflict and class politics in the United States. Consider that in 1848—the year the war with Mexico ended—workers in multiple countries across Europe revolted, built barricades, established labor parties and unions, and called for "the social-democratization of European politics."[7] The United States had its share of hungry, exploited workers, but "instead of waging class war upward—on aristocrats and owners," white workers "waged race war outward, on the frontier." Young workers, Grandin writes, "didn't head to the barricades to fight the gentry" but rather "joined with the gentry to go west and fight Indians and Mexicans."[8] Exploring the conjoined histories of the frontier and the border allows us to see how this racialized legacy of legal and extrajudicial violence has shaped American conceptions of freedom, sovereignty, democracy, citizenship, and the law.[9] The history of anti-Mexican politics

---

certainly "central to Anglo identity," whiteness was both "complicated and contested in eighteenth- and nineteenth-century Texas," with some ethnic Mexicans and "elite and light-skinned Mexicans" claiming whiteness even while experiencing "social, political, and economic marginalization." In this way, the term *Anglo* supplements the language of whiteness, serving as a "historically descriptive" way to mark the "racialized divide that developed in Texas and the rest of the Southwest as English-speaking whites poured in and worked to establish dominance over ethnic Mexicans." See Mark Allan Goldberg, *Conquering Sickness: Race, Health, and Colonization in the Texas Borderlands* (Lincoln: University of Nebraska Press, 2016), xix.

6. Grandin, *End of the Myth*, 85.

7. Grandin, 94–95.

8. Grandin, 95.

9. In claiming that a significant portion of conservatives exhibit intense affective reactions against Latinx citizens and noncitizens, I am hardly saying that Latinos are the *only* population facing visceral political, racial, and cultural hostility from the Right. Anti-Muslim hysteria is clearly producing particular forms of racialized hate speech and violent xenophobia, as seen in the ongoing efforts of the Trump administration to

illuminates how racialized violence continues to influence today's aggressive nativist politics.

The war concluded in 1848 with the signing of the Treaty of Guadalupe Hidalgo, which officially recognized the U.S. annexation of Texas and ceded to the United States one-third of Mexico's territory, including all or part of what would later become California, Arizona, Nevada, Utah, Wyoming, Colorado, Kansas, Oklahoma, and New Mexico, in return for a $15 million payment.[10] The treaty created a two-thousand-mile southern border and transferred to the United States a total of some half million square miles. The land was home to eighty thousand to one hundred thousand people, a diverse population that included "old-line Spanish families, who could trace their land claims back generations, centuries even; their mestizo and mulatto servants and ranch hands, along with other laborers, thousands of migrants in California, prospecting for gold;

---

ban individuals from a variety of countries in Africa and the Middle East. We've seen an increase in anti-Semitic incidents; anti-Asian sentiments are increasingly visible (ranging from long-standing anti-Asian hostility aimed at China and Japan to the racism against South Asians that often merges into Islamophobia). Transphobic and misogynist policies attacking the rights of women and sexual minorities have been frequent and ongoing. And of course, anti-Blackness and settler colonialism represent two of the most foundational and dominant racial logics circulating both historically and today. In placing Mexicans at the center of my analysis, I am not calling on political theorists to replace the Black–white binary with a new racial hierarchy that erases or sidelines the significance of other populations and histories. Instead, this book is a call for developing deeper and more specific knowledge of the various populations that make up the American racial order. In this instance, rather than the all-too-common references to the racial subordination of "Blacks and Latinos," scholars should move beyond such cursory generalizations and instead provide deeper analyses of the *specific* historical and political dynamics occurring within various racialized populations. See Smith, "Heteropatriarchy and the Three Pillars of White Supremacy"; see also Bebout, *Whiteness on the Border,* 11.

10. Including Texas, Mexico lost more than half its territory in the war. See Gutiérrez, *Walls and Mirrors,* 13.

and scores of indigenous peoples, including Apache, Navajo, Pueblo, Ute, Yaqui, and Tohono O'odham."[11]

The war made the United States a continental power while exacerbating tensions between free and slave states. And while the war led to the nation gaining a staggering amount of new territory, some American expansionists had hoped for an even *larger* seizure of land. As David Gutiérrez notes, both during and before the war, many Americans had argued that the United States should aim to annex the whole of Mexico "and perhaps South America as well."[12] Prior to war, the "All-Mexico" movement made its case in political speeches, newspaper editorials, travelogues, and memoirs.[13] Describing in 1836 the reasons why Americans should support the colonists and Tejanos rebelling against the Mexican government, William H. Wharton—a diplomat, statesman, and advocate for Texas's complete independence from Mexico—argued that a just and benevolent God would forbid that Texas "again become a howling wilderness, trod only by savages" and "permanently benighted by the ignorance and superstition, the anarchy

11. Grandin, *End of the Myth*, 92, 94.

12. Gutiérrez, *Walls and Mirrors*, 14. For further discussion of the All-Mexico movement, see Frederick Merk, *Manifest Destiny and Mission in American History* (New York: Vintage, 1963), 107–43, and David Pletcher, *The Diplomacy of Annexation: Texas, Oregon, and the Mexican War* (Columbia: University of Missouri Press, 1973), 522–26, 551–52, 555–57, 561.

13. As David Gutiérrez notes in *Walls and Mirrors*, in the popular 1840 adventure travelogue *Two Years before the Mast*, author Richard Henry Dana strongly influenced American popular perceptions of northern Mexican society by painting "an unflattering portrait of Californios" as "thriftless, proud . . . of little education . . . and none of the best morality." Gutiérrez 18–19. But alongside his disparagement of the population, Dana's enthusiasm regarding the territory Mexicans inhabited was clear: describing "'California's four or five hundred miles of sea-coast, . . . good harbors, . . . fine forests, . . . and herds of cattle,' Dana was moved to wonder, 'In the hands of an enterprising people, what a country this might be!'" See Dana, *Two Years before the Mast* (1940; repr., New York: Airmont, 1966), 136, 137; see also Gutiérrez, *Walls and Mirrors*, 18–19.

and rapine of Mexican misrule."[14] Describing the task of Texas settlement, Wharton characterizes it as a project that is as racial as it is republican:

> The Anglo-American race are destined to be for ever the proprietors of this land of *promise* and *fulfilment*. *Their* laws will govern it, *their* learning will enlighten it, their enterprise will improve it. *Their* flocks will range its boundless pastures, for *them* its fertile lands will yield their luxuriant harvests; its beauteous rivers will waft the products of *their* industry and enterprise . . . in the possession of homes fortified by the genius of liberty, and sanctified by the spirit of a beneficent and tolerant religion. . . . The wilderness of Texas has been redeemed by Anglo-American blood and enterprise. The colonists have carried with them the language, the habits, and the lofty love of liberty that has always characterized and distinguished their ancestors.[15]

Wharton's words exemplify Olson's point that "racial subordination" both "constructs democratic ideals as well as violates them." In the case of Mexico, we can see how white supremacy limits the possibilities for full democracy while making white democracy possible. For Wharton, the language of white supremacy is enmeshed in the civic language of liberty, popular sovereignty, industry, and religious tolerance. Similarly, describing Anglo settlement in Mexican territory, *New York Herald* editor James Gordon Bennett extols how "healthy, vigorous republics, unknown and undreamt of among the threadbare dynasties of the old world, have sprung up and flourished with a prospect of healthy permanency."[16] Yet Bennett also warns that "wherever the experiment of democratic governance has succeeded, it is only in cases where the distinct purity of the Caucasian race has been preserved unmixed with the lower orders of humanity."[17]

14. William H. Wharton, "Address on Texas Independence," *Magazine of History* 22, no. 4 (1922): 236.

15. Wharton, emphasis original.

16. James Gordon Bennett, "Is the Mexican War Ended?," *New York Herald*, June 5, 1846.

17. Bennett.

In these depictions of Anglo-American "promise and fulfillment," we can see what Bebout has characterized as "whiteness on the border"—the "discursive and ideological constellation in which representations of Mexico, Mexicans, and Mexican Americans are deployed to construct . . . white identity as American identity."[18] Whiteness on the border reveals a linkage "between the U.S.–Mexican border region and imaginings of U.S. national racial identity."[19] Moreover, as Bebout notes, this vivid imaginary of the Mexican Other is a "long-enduring, prevalent, and dynamic component of the U.S. racial project."[20]

Waging war and settling Mexican lands gave white settlers new opportunities to enact frontier freedom and embody the sovereign will of the people—to struggle and strive; to subdue and inhabit "new" lands, seek wealth, acquire property, establish new communities, spread "civilization," and replace Mexican misrule with "vigorous republics" and "free institutions of Anglo Americans," creating new spaces of white self-governance—all while creating new opportunities for themselves and their families.[21] These mass-based, participatory projects, designed to counter the "despotism" of Mexican politics with the free institutions of the United States, highlight how Mexican conquest was an expression of both white supremacy and popular will, allowing whites to act and claim their right on behalf of "the people" to exercise power and enact their identity as Americans.

Frontier freedom on the border was also a project invested in rescuing the region from both Indians and Mexicans. Serving a double function, conquest also saved the region from "Mexican misrule"—a failure of governance defined in part by Mexico's inability to eliminate the presence of indigeneity, turning the territory into a "howling wilderness, trod only by savages." As Laura

18. Bebout, *Whiteness on the Border,* 2.
19. Bebout, 24.
20. Bebout, 71.
21. See De León, *They Called Them Greasers,* 1, 3–5.

Gomez has written, both Mexicans and Indigenous communities contended with a form of "double colonization" that imposed a system of status inequalities grounded in racial difference.[22] Forced to navigate two different racial regimes simultaneously, the combination of conquest alongside the imposition of U.S. law upon a preexisting Spanish and Mexican colonial racial order created complex new racial dynamics for both populations. As Gomez has demonstrated, a central paradox of 1848 was "the *legal* construction of Mexicans as racially 'white' alongside the *social* construction of Mexicans as non-white and as racially inferior."[23] Following 1848, Mexican elites "accommodated, contested, and negotiated their position" in this new American racial order.[24] At times, this process involved claiming white status and distancing themselves from alliances with tribal populations. As Gomez notes, in places such as New Mexico, American colonizers were able to co-opt those Mexican Americans willing to trade on their mestizo, part-European heritage to "divide Mexican Americans from their Pueblo neighbors."[25] In sum, both the Spanish and the American racial systems sought to enlist Mexicans in the management of the territories, leading Mexicans to become "agents in the reproduction of racial subordination" even as they were victims of it.[26] Moreover, as María Josefina Saldaña-Portillo suggests, Mexicans' political and racial identities are rooted in racially produced geographies of colonial governance that were mediated by notions of indigeneity and "Indianness" developed under Spanish, Mexican, and U.S. rule.[27] The Mexican-American War and its aftermath created an "infelicitous boundary between indigenous and Mexican" racial identities.[28] Even before the American war against Mexico,

22. Gomez, *Manifest Destinies,* 49.
23. Gomez, 5
24. Gomez, 5.
25. Gomez, 119.
26. Gomez, 121.
27. Saldaña-Portillo, *Indian Given,* 8.
28. Saldaña-Portillo, 191.

"it was Mexicans' 'half-bred' status, their barbarous core, that required U.S. conquest for the proper administration of the frontier." Anglo settlers saw the frontier as "horribly mismanaged" and in need of rescue to "release its democratic potential and develop its indigenous resources."[29] Yet it was envisioning the incorporation of ever "larger numbers of non-white, non-English speaking people into the United States" that ultimately tempered expansionists' claims to Mexico's territory.[30]

In each of these depictions, we can see how emerging tropes regarding the "Mexican character" came to the fore. Latinx scholars Leo Chavez, Arnoldo De León, and Bebout identify at least four tropes about Mexico, Mexicans, and Mexican Americans that organized Anglo attitudes and underwrote Anglo actions. In these tropes, Mexicans were scripted as "indolent, morally defective, un-American, and savagely violent."[31] Moreover, as Lee Bebout puts it, "if Mexicans are lazy, disloyal, savage, and immoral, then whites 'as mirror opposites' are hardworking, loyal, civilized, and moral beings—ideal citizen subjects."[32]

The power of these racialized images and assumptions had a significant impact on how the United States approached Mexican land annexation and political incorporation. As historian Reginald Horsman shows, the dispute about annexing Mexican territory was less an argument about territory than one about Mexicans.[33] Charles Bent, the first civilian governor of the territory of New Mexico, proclaimed that "the Mexican character is made up of

29. Saldaña-Portillo, 225.

30. Gutiérrez, *Walls and Mirrors,* 15.

31. Bebout, *Whiteness on the Borders,* 42.

32. Bebout, 43.

33. Reginald Horsman, *Race and Manifest Destiny: The Origins of American Racial Anglo-Saxonism* (Cambridge, Mass.: Harvard University Press, 1981), 238–39. Horsman highlights editorials from Whig newspapers, summing up their argument against annexing Mexican territory: "Why should the national character be sullied by the use of force or the population diluted by alien ingredients?"

stupidity, obstinacy, ignorance, duplicity, and vanity"; Edward Hannegan, an All-Mexico U.S. senator from Indiana, characterized Mexicans as "utterly unfit for the blessings and restraints of rational liberty, because they cannot comprehend the distinction between regulated freedom, and the unbridled licentiousness which consults only the evil passions of the human heart."[34] In a similar vein, John C. Calhoun, Andrew Jackson's former vice president and eventual U.S. senator from South Carolina, argued against incorporation, asserting that Mexicans represented an amalgamation of "impure races, not [even] as good as the Cherokees or Choctaws." Calhoun asked, "Can we incorporate a people so dissimilar to us in every aspect—so little qualified for free and popular government—without certain destruction to our political institutions?"[35]

For men such as Bent, Hannegan, and Calhoun, incorporating a large number of Mexicans into the United States would create a demographic shift so disruptive as to destroy American political institutions, leading to a crisis of sovereignty. Conquest had the potential to turn "the people" into an amalgamation of "impure races" who were "utterly unfit" to exercise sovereign power. Such depictions of Mexicans rendered them outside the scope of popular sovereignty—such subjects could never be part of "the people," subjects whose consent was necessary to authorize the power of the state and its government. Nor were such portrayals of Mexicans unusual at the time—such characterizations were familiar to Americans through wartime accounts in newspapers, colonial historiographies, and political writings. In the period 1821–45, writers routinely described Mexican natives as a form of "degraded humanity"—"uncivilized" and "beastly."[36] In contrast to the

34. Grandin, *End of the Myth*, 92.

35. *Congressional Globe*, 29th Cong., 2nd sess., February 9, 1848, appendix, 327, and *Congressional Globe*, 30th Cong., 1st sess., January 4, 1848, 98–99, quoted in Horsman, *Race and Manifest Destiny*, 241. See also Gutiérrez, *Walls and Mirrors*, 16.

36. De León, *They Called Them Greasers*, 5.

romanticized stereotypes of certain Indigenous populations, annexed Mexicans were often depicted as "kissing cousins" to the fictitious *indio bárbaros*—subjects lingering in "dangerous proximity to an imputed savage Indian difference."[37] Emerging during moments of "colonial or national crisis," the racial imaginary of "Indians" and the "*indios bárbaros*" are part of colonial legacies that characterize certain forms of indigeneity as both lawless and monstrous.[38] In the U.S. imperialist imagination, the "indio bárbaro of the borderlands" is a subject who "roams and raids and kills without mercy"—a figure who must be "excised not simply from the geographical borders of nation, but from the very boundaries of humanity."[39] Such portrayals of "Mexican depravity and violence" represent an assemblage of "lasting stereotypes" that continue to influence the contemporary politics of race and immigration in the United States.[40] The trope of the violent, savage Mexican has yet to dissipate because "it serves so many functions," particularly in its ability to "justify and obscure white violence."[41]

37. Saldaña-Portillo, *Indian Given,* 156, 203.

38. Saldaña-Portillo, 9.

39. Saldaña-Portillo, 376. Importantly, Saldaña-Portillo shows that in the colonial record of New Spain, *indios bárbaros* was a more fluid category than the fixed idea of barbarism that emerges following U.S. conquest: "bárbaros, like the term Chichimecas for the Nahaus, also indicated a nomadic incivility, a heathen recalcitrance. The Nahuas had considered these northern tribes who resisted incorporation into their empire. . . . Nevertheless . . . for Spanish administrators and vecinos of the northern frontier, indios bárbaros existed on a continuum of Christian unity, of Catholic humanity, not outside of it. Indios bárbaros could be friends and allies, or mortal enemies, but the steadfast intent of Spanish Empire was to bring them (by persuasion or force) under the mantle of Christian dominion. . . . Bárbaro's condition was considered remediable, capable of shifting from recalcitrant foreigner to intimate relation. . . . Unlike their Anglo-American counterparts for whom Indian savagery came to signify an inevitable vanishing from the scene/seen of empire and nation, for the Spaniards the indios bárbaros filled the landscape with the promise of colonial mission." See Saldaña-Portillo, 154–55.

40. Gutiérrez, *Walls and Mirrors,* 20.

41. Bebout, *Whiteness on the Border,* 62.

According to historian Arnoldo De León, during the Texas Revolution, colonists fighting their war of independence from Mexico spoke alarmingly of "savage, degenerate, half-civilized, and barbarous Mexicans committing massacres and atrocities at Goliad and the Alamo."[42] At times, the Mexican threat took on a sexual dimension, as Anglo political leaders invoked images of Mexican rapists laying claim not only to land but to the bodies of their female family members. Texas settler and judge John W. Hall asked the American public to "imagine what would happen if Mexican soldiers gained a foothold" in Texas—"beloved wives, mothers, daughters, sisters, and helpless innocent children would be given up to the dire pollution . . . of the barbarians."[43]

Interestingly, the manner in which the U.S. Army waged the Mexican-American War not only encouraged violence but made it intrinsic to border politics. The war was fought in an extremely decentralized manner, with officers "barely exercising control over their troops. In other words, soldiers experienced the violence they committed—the 'repetition of the most heinous offenses, murder, rapine, robbery, and rape,' as one newspaper wrote of U.S. atrocities committed on Mexicans—as a form of liberty."[44] Anglos who shifted from being soldiers to settlers often carried this "blood-soaked entitlement" with them—indeed, "popular sovereignty" shifted from being "a rallying cry for settlers who wanted to be free of federal control"[45] to, as historian Paul Foos puts it, a "synonym for racist brutality and wanton usurpation."[46] The history of the Texas Rangers reflects this ongoing dynamic of Mexicans at the border being subject to practices that continually

42. De León, *They Called Them Greasers,* 11.
43. De León, 10–11.
44. Grandin, *End of the Myth,* 98.
45. Grandin, 98.
46. Paul Foos, *A Short, Offhand, Killing Affair: Soldiers and Social Conflict during the Mexican-American War* (Chapel Hill: University of North Carolina Press, 2003), 175.

blur the lines between "enforcing state laws, practicing vigilantism, and inciting racial terror."[47]

In short, during the Herrenvolk era of white democracy, law enforcement agencies such as the Texas Rangers—codifying settlers' practices—created a set of expectations for white citizens regarding how the law should operate and relate to Mexican populations. The legacy of this violent and racialized approach to the law can be seen in the treatment of migrants at the border and in contemporary practices of migrant arrest and detention.

Conquest and the Politics of Disappearance

Alongside popular depictions of Mexican savagery, unassimilable difference, and calls for the violent subjugation of Mexicans, other forms of white supremacy envisioned bringing enlightenment to a backward people in need of advancement. As Arnoldo De León notes, Anglo settlers saw themselves as "freedom loving frontiersmen" who entertained "a strong belief in themselves and the superiority of their way of life."[48] Supporters of the All-Mexico movement stated that Mexicans "would 'learn to love her ravishers,'" while columnist and editor John O'Sullivan argued that the influx of white Americans into recently conquered territory would lead to both uplift and absorption.[49] In his 1845 declaration of "manifest destiny," O'Sullivan described an "irresistible army of Anglo-Saxon[s]" bringing with them "the plough and the rifle . . . schools and colleges, courts and representative halls, mills and meeting-houses,"[50] that would ultimately lead Mexicans to "simply melt into American society as they experienced the ben-

47. Grandin, *End of the Myth,* 11.

48. De León, *They Called Them Greasers,* 2.

49. Grandin, *End of the Myth,* 151.

50. John O'Sullivan, "Annexation," *United States Magazine and Democratic Review* 17, no. 1 (July–August 1845).

efits of American civilization."[51] Describing the "Mexican race" as "perfectly accustomed to being conquered," an 1847 *New York Sun* editorial echoed O'Sullivan by asserting that "the only new lesson we shall teach is that our victories will give liberty, safety, and prosperity to the vanquished. . . . To *liberate* and *ennoble* . . . not to *enslave* and *debase*—is our mission."[52]

Notwithstanding this language of uplift and absorption, anxieties about incorporating large numbers of Mexicans into the United States ultimately led lawmakers to emphasize America's territorial acquisition while downplaying the impact of Mexicans joining the American polity. The consensus view regarding the incorporation of Mexican territory and people could be summed up by Michigan senator Lewis Cass, who insisted, "We do not want the people of Mexico, either as citizens or subjects. All we want is a portion of territory, which they nominally hold, generally uninhabited, or where inhabited at all, sparsely so, and with a population, which would recede, or identify itself with ours."[53] The possessive logic of white democracy was further strengthened by the postwar discovery of gold in California and silver deposits in Nevada and New Mexico—discoveries that offered Mexicans few opportunities. The discovery of gold led to passage of a Foreign Miners Tax that led to the expulsion of not only Mexican and Latin American prospectors but Mexican Americans.[54] Moreover, the rapid and ongoing influx of white settlers—in addition to the transplantation of a new political and legal system—displaced many landowning Mexicans from their property.

Such racialized territorial dispossession promised white citizens a chance at newfound forms of wealth and mobility, allowing

51. Gutiérrez, *Walls and Mirrors,* 15.

52. Gutiérrez, 15.

53. *Congressional Globe,* 29th Cong., 2nd sess., February 10, 1847, 191, quoted in Horseman, *Race and Manifest Destiny,* 241; Gutiérrez, *Walls and Mirrors,* 16.

54. Gutiérrez, *Walls and Mirrors,* 19.

them to enlarge their own "areas of freedom." As Grandin notes, during this era, "war became an even more effective venue of social mobility." Between 1850 and 1855, Congress was "suddenly the executor of a near-entire continent" that it now had the power to "dispense" and distribute to white citizens. Veterans of the Mexican campaign were promised "bounty land" for their service. This annexation of new territory led veterans of previous wars—many of whom had been promised but never received similar bounties—also to demand compensation.[55] At that point, Congress "overwhelmingly passed a series of laws that granted land to *all* veterans of *any* past war, going back to 1790. Hundreds of thousands of veterans, or their widows and heirs, received warrants for over thirty-four million acres." If veterans didn't want the land, "they could redeem the warrants for cash."[56]

Here again, we see how the language of conquest and annexation depicts Mexicans as having something of value (land, gold, silver) while characterizing their presence as an obstacle to be overcome. Manifest destiny gave Anglo-Americans not only a fierce sense of entitlement over seemingly boundless lands and resources but a belief in their inherent right to dominate and/or disappear the inhabitants of these recently acquired lands. Following the war, Mexicans were often depicted as "disappearing"—Mexicans would either self-deport and "recede" into Mexico or lose their "Mexican character" by experiencing the "ennobling" benefits of American civilization and citizenship and engaging in a process of "unbecoming Mexican."[57] Indeed, Mexicans were often de-

55. Grandin, *End of the Myth,* 97.
56. Grandin, 97.
57. Saldaña-Portillo, *Indian Given,* 195. As Saldaña-Portillo notes, article 9 of the Treaty of Guadalupe Hidalgo states the following:

> Article 9: "The Mexicans who, in the territories aforesaid, *shall not preserve the character of citizens of the Mexican Republic* . . . shall be incorporated into the Union of the United States and be admitted, at the proper time (to be judged of by the Congress of the United States)

picted as a population so debased that their survival in the context of Anglo domination seemed highly unlikely. Describing the Mexicans and their presumed fate, *New York Herald* editor James Gordon Bennett declared,

> Sluggish inertness and intellectual imbecility are the unhappy characteristics of the race . . . emasculated and totally incapable of self government. . . . It is now the manifest destiny of this republic to extend its empire and civilization over the rich and fertile plains of Mexico. . . . The tide of emigration will set towards Mexico, and the imbecile race that now inhabits that country is as sure to melt away at the approach of Anglo-Saxon energy and enterprise as snow before a southern sun. Their fate will be similar to that of the Indians of this country—the race, before a century rolls over us, will become extinct.[58]

In sum, despite their differences, Wharton, Dana, Bent, Hannegan, Calhoun, O'Sullivan, Cass, and Bennett shared a belief that the incorporation of Mexicans and Mexican territory would not—and should not—alter the nature and character of the United States.

> to the enjoyment of all the rights of the citizens of the United States according to the principles of the Constitution; and in the mean time shall be maintained and protected in the free enjoyment of their liberty and property, and secured in the free exercise of their religion without restriction" (193, emphasis added).

Citing early American scholar David Kazanjian, Saldaña-Portillo writes, "The fulfillment of the promise of article 9 formally required Mexicans to give up, to relinquish, the 'character' of Mexicanness in order to enjoy 'all the rights of the citizens of the United States' promised by the treaty. As the first sentence of article 9 stipulates in the prohibition 'shall not preserve the character,' Kazanjian suggests, 'the first step on the road to becoming a U.S. citizen is a negation, a becoming un-preserved, disposed of, lost, wasted' (2003, 207). Becoming a U.S. citizen required the loss of a Mexican character that is at once national and racial, as the vernacular use of 'character' underscores." See David Kazanjian, *The Colonizing Trick: National Culture and Imperial Citizenship in Early America* (Minneapolis: University of Minnesota Press, 2003), and Saldaña-Portillo, *Indian Given*, 194.

58. Bennett, "Is the Mexican War Ended?"

Together, the logic of manifest destiny and settler sovereignty meant that "the people" would remain white. Whether for or against the greater annexation of Mexican territory, what these authors shared was the presumption that Mexicans were fundamentally a people of inferior status—potentially valuable as a source of labor but unequipped for liberal citizenship, a population whose cultural and racial deficiencies would be counteracted through assimilation and the loss of their "Mexican character" or whose position within U.S. society would (rightly) be limited, subsidiary, and subordinate in nature. Not surprisingly, in the two decades following conquest, Mexican Americans found themselves relegated to a "stigmatized, subordinate position" throughout the Southwest.[59]

At the same time, as Laura Gomez has demonstrated, in granting naturalization rights to white persons, the Treaty of Guadalupe Hidalgo promoted a *legal* definition of Mexicans as "white" yet "socially" defined as nonwhite.[60] This racial indeterminacy had the paradoxical effect of making racialized violence against Mexicans both more justifiable and more defensible. Because Latinos have a historically ambiguous relationship to whiteness, Herrenvolk attacks on Mexicans were legitimated through depicting them as enemy soldiers, bandits, or revolutionaries—violent, duplicitous, criminal, and unfit for citizenship.

During the war, officials and pundits reassured white citizens that the nature and character of the United States would remain constant no matter the eventual borders, so it is no surprise that the dream of white settlers in the Southwest was one of absence, absorption, and exploitability. This desire was complicated by the fact that Mexicans who found themselves on the American side of the new border were eligible for citizenship, yet that access to membership came with enduring racial tropes of Mexicans as suspect subjects, potential threats to the nation's cultural, economic,

59. Gutiérrez, *Walls and Mirrors,* 21.
60. Gomez, *Manifest Destinies,* 87.

and civic character. Continually characterized as an ambivalently indigenous *other*—savage, lawless, and invasive—the history of Mexican incorporation through war and conquest produced a complex, contested, and violent legacy for Mexican American political membership. Despite the claims of the Treaty of Guadalupe Hidalgo, white politicians, journalists, military leaders, ranchers, and business interests never articulated a vision of shared membership in which Mexican American citizens and Anglos would collectively rule each other as equals. That was never the vision. Instead, Anglos invoked long-standing racist tropes characterizing Latinos as violent, criminal, duplicitous, and civically unfit; the promise of 1848 reflected a long-standing desire for labor and land, while imagining Mexicans as a removable population that could be treated instrumentally.

Of course, the problem for Anglos in the Southwest is that Mexicans did *not* disappear. Mexicans continued to own land and to defend their legal access to property. They continued to compete for economic opportunities in sectors like agriculture and mining.[61] In sum, not only did Mexicans endure as a visible and purposeful presence on their land and in their communities but they continued to migrate and claim social, political, and cultural space. For Anglo settlers who never wanted Mexicans as equal members of the polity in the first place, their ongoing (and growing) presence is the broken promise of white democracy. Unsurprisingly, a racialized dynamic emerged in which Mexicans and other Latinos (even when native born) were viewed as "immigrant-citizens" and "foreigners with U.S. citizenship," questionable subjects whose political membership was continually suspect and often resented.[62]

61. For more on the relationship between economics, racial prejudice, and mob violence, see William D. Carrigan and Clive Webb, *Forgotten Dead: Mob Violence against Mexicans in the United States* (New York: Oxford University Press, 2013), 33–51.

62. Lorrin Thomas, *Puerto Rican Citizen: History and Political Identity in Twentieth-Century New York City* (Chicago: University of Chicago Press, 2010), 3.

Frontier Justice: The Herrenvolk Legacy of the Texas Rangers

Following the Texas Revolution and the Mexican-American War, most Anglo settlers saw Mexicans as belonging to "a different, inferior race" that warranted segregation and discrimination.[63] Yet, following the war and into the early twentieth century, Mexican migration was subject to virtually no restrictions, with Mexicans and Americans free to move across the border. Despite being exempt from immigration quotas, Mexican nationals migrating north to escape the economic depression and downturns of the 1870s and 1880s were met with hostility and violence. Throughout the 1910s, the violence increased further as refugees fleeing the Mexican Revolution were met with growing nativist sentiment and denied humanitarian aid. According to historians William Carrigan and Clive Webb, "from the California Gold Rush to the last recorded instance of a Mexican lynched in public in 1928, vigilantes hanged, burned, and shot thousands of persons of Mexican descent in the United States."[64] During this period, the figure of the "menacing" Mexican revolutionary and bandit was cemented in the popular imaginary as a figure who could be killed with impunity. Moreover, any local resident who looked Mexican, regardless of citizenship, social status, or evidence of guilt, could be profiled as a "bandit" or "bandit sympathizer."[65]

Guided by a Herrenvolk conception of freedom that understood white citizens as having "saved" the region from Mexicans, a growing sense of economic competition led to increased forms of violence against the growing number of Mexicans in the United States. Indeed, according to American studies scholar Monica Muñoz Martinez, "between 1848 and 1928 in Texas alone, 232 eth-

63. Grandin, *End of the Myth,* 193.
64. Carrigan and Webb, *Forgotten Dead,* 1.
65. See Villanueva, *Lynching of Mexicans,* 105, and Carrigan and Webb, *Forgotten Dead,* 65.

nic Mexicans were lynched by vigilante groups of three or more people."[66] Mexican lynching victims often died together in small groups because mobs often targeted groups of Mexicans rather than individuals.[67] With local authorities and deputized citizens playing a particularly conspicuous role in mob violence against Mexicans, such violence often took place in broad daylight, in the presence of witnesses and prominent citizens.

Indeed, as Amy Wood has written, members of lynch mobs understood themselves not as criminals or defilers of the law but as "honorable vindicators of justice and popular sovereignty, fulfilling their rights as citizens to punish crimes against their communities." Mobs expected and anticipated that their violence would be noticed and made public. The "tremendous symbolic power" of lynchings existed precisely because such events were visually sensational. In this way, such rituals of violence were performed not only to create a sense of racial terror in nonwhite subjects but as "spectacles for other whites," designed to "instill and perpetuate a sense of racial supremacy in their white spectators."[68] Drawing on a tradition of white democracy that allowed citizens to both wield and exceed the law, the history of the Texas Rangers reflects this political legacy of treating Mexicans with impunity—ignoring the distinction between citizen and noncitizen and blurring the lines between vigilantism, state law, and racial terror.

Popular accounts of the Rangers—organized in 1823 by Stephen F. Austin to "protect settlers and their property"—describe them as starting off as "a small group of men" committed to "upholding values of law and order and justice," while "protecting their friends and their family members from Indian raids."[69] Yet, as

66. Monica Muñoz Martinez, *The Injustice Never Leaves You: Anti-Mexican Violence in Texas* (Cambridge, Mass.: Harvard University Press, 2018), 6.

67. Carrigan and Webb, *Forgotten Dead,* 75.

68. Wood, *Lynching and Spectacle,* 24, 1–2.

69. Martinez, *Injustice Never Leaves You,* 10, 254.

scholars have shown, the Rangers often served as a fighting force created by Anglo settlers in the ongoing war for racial supremacy. According to Kelly Lytle Hernández, the Texas Rangers "battled indigenous groups for dominance in the region, chased down runaway slaves who struck for freedom deep within Mexico, and settled scores with anyone who challenged the Anglo-American project in Texas."[70]

Turned into an official branch of law enforcement in 1902, the first two decades of the twentieth century saw hundreds of new Texas Rangers patrolling the region—by 1918, the force had grown to approximately 1,350 Rangers. Existing at the intersection of vigilante violence and state and military policing, one reason vigilantism targeting Mexicans intensified between 1915 to 1919 was because "duly appointed law officers played such a prominent role in leading and encouraging the era's numerous extralegal executions."[71] During the peak of anti-Mexican violence, Rangers often invoked *la ley de fuga,* the law of flight or escape, authorizing officials to kill any person who ran or resisted arrest. As Martinez notes, it was common knowledge that Rangers "released prisoners and ordered them to run. Officers then proceeded to shoot the prisoner while in flight, later filing reports that they killed the prisoner to prevent escape or because the prisoner resisted arrest."[72] With no way for authorities to refute the claim that the victim struggled or fled, *la ley de fuga* "gave Rangers near-limitless power to kill."[73]

As scholars of the Rangers have rightly noted, making sense of a culture of impunity that allowed anti-Mexican violence to thrive in Texas requires acknowledging the ongoing history of anti-

70. Kelly Lytle Hernández, *Migra! A History of the U.S. Border Patrol* (Berkeley: University of California Press, 2010), 20.

71. Carrigan and Webb, *Forgotten Dead,* 84.

72. Martinez, *Injustice Never Leaves You,* 11, 90.

73. See Lily Meyer, "The Texas Ranger: Good Guys No More," *Los Angeles Review of Books,* October 31, 2018.

Black violence in the state. As a state built by conquest and slavery, its history shows that anti-Black and anti-Mexican violence mutually reinforced one another. Moreover, Texas Rangers who abused their power targeted both ethnic Mexicans and African Americans. Martinez observes,

> Of all the states in the union, Texas maintained a national profile for having a long and rampant history of lynching. In 1918 alone, Texas mobs lynched eleven victims, second only to Georgia, where mobs claimed nineteen victims. In 1919, when the NAACP released a list of the top ten states with the highest rates of lynching since 1889, Texas came in third with 335 victims, behind Georgia and Mississippi.[74]

Entwined with a mythology of the frontier, in the context of Herrenvolk democracy, Anglo settlers saw no contradiction between the rule of law and extrajudicial conduct against Mexicans. A particularly horrific example of white democracy's claiming of law while killing with impunity is the 1918 Porvenir massacre, when Texas Rangers, along with soldiers from the U.S. Cavalry and local ranchers, murdered fifteen unarmed Mexicans ranging in age from sixteen to sixty-four.[75] Later that year, the Texas courts denied survivors any sort of legal, financial, or even symbolic redress by failing to prosecute the Rangers and civilians who participated in the massacre. Nor was the Porvenir massacre unprecedented—in 1919, at least thirty-four victims "were removed from the custody of officers, taken either in transport or from jails."[76]

74. Martinez, *Injustice Never Leaves You,* 178.

75. Martinez, 122; see also Carrigan and Webb, *Forgotten Dead,* 64; Villanueva, *Lynching of Mexicans,* 103–4.

76. Martinez, *Injustice Never Leaves You,* 175. To drive home the legally sanctioned nature of the violence, in 1919, when Texas state representative José Tomás Canales (the state's sole Hispanic representative at the time) set up a joint committee to probe the Rangers' criminal conduct, defenders claimed that Texas Rangers were justified in using any violent means necessary to protect white Americans, arguing that opponents of such actions had no grasp on the volatile climate at the border. Congressman Claude Benton Hudspeth, a former Ranger, advocated for local residents taking the law into their own hands, arguing that "you

As with African Americans, violence against Mexicans was imprinted onto the public imaginary through the circulation of photographs and postcards showing images of torture and death. With amateur photography emerging alongside the heyday of lynching, between the 1880s and the 1930s, images of Black men and women lynched by white mobs were regularly sold and circulated. In the case of Mexicans, the revolutionary upheaval in Mexico provided a rich subject for photographs on both sides of the border. Such images helped establish a frontier aesthetic whose racist iconography remains visible to this day.

As Martinez reminds us, American photographs of Mexican corpses did not portray the dead as victims so much as "a symbol of progress": the photographs were offered as evidence of American superiority and military power. More dead Mexican bodies on the U.S.–Mexican border meant "safer conditions for Anglo settlement, consumption, and capital."[77] Amateurs and entrepreneurs both documented and sold images of lynched Mexican men, decomposing corpses, and military prisoners lined up prior to execution. Often American soldiers were photographed "grinning while posing with dead or wounded Mexican prisoners of war."[78] Even more significantly, Texas Rangers, local police, U.S. soldiers, and civilians are shown in these photos.

As scholars of lynching photography have demonstrated, the availability of these postcards for purchase and casual exchange

---

cannot handle those Mexicans with kid gloves, not when they come twelve miles below El Paso and steal a milk cow every night or two. . . . I don't believe in murdering people, but there are a bad class of men along the River that have to be handled in a certain way." For Hudspeth and many of his colleagues, state brutality was a necessary means for dealing with Mexicans who were criminal by nature. Despite their legal training, Hudspeth and others described Mexican residents as not having the legal protections or rights guaranteed to American citizens and foreign nationals. See Martinez, 208–9, 211.

77. Martinez, 235.

78. Martinez, 233.

was not created to encourage a public reckoning with the evils of racialized violence. Instead, photographs depicting mob violence were, more often than not, printed and sold to *celebrate* such violence, offering its white viewers and recipients "a titillating glimpse of life on the border."[79] Selling and circulating these images ensured that the moment of racial terror survived long after the event. Photographs served as "a bonding mechanism for those who shared the images and a continued method of racial intimidation."[80] An example is the 1877 photograph *Hanged at the Water Street Bridge*. Taken in Santa Cruz, California, the image shows the lynched bodies of José Chamales and Francisco Arias. As Carrigan and Webb note, although the two Mexican victims were hanged at 2:00 A.M., the photo was taken during daylight hours, "meaning the corpses had been suspended for many hours." That these spectators—"suit-wearing men and barefooted boys"—did not cut down the bodies but instead called for and then posed for a photographer "says much about the culture of lynching in Santa Cruz in 1877."[81]

Photographs such as *Hanged at the Water Street Bridge* illustrate how acts of torture were sanctioned by white citizens, who saw their participation and presence in these images as authorizing extralegal forms of justice. In this way, we are reminded of Ida B. Wells-Barnett's insight regarding the profoundly *public* character of lynchings, noting that hundreds (and sometimes thousands) of people witnessed these murders. Indeed, as Amy Wood argues, it is the act of "witnessing" that underlies the particular form spectatorship linked to the practice of lynching. For Wood, to act as a witness is to "play a public role, one that bestows a particular kind

79. Martinez, 233. See also Ken Gonzales-Day, *Lynching in the West: 1850–1935* (Durham, N.C.: Duke University Press, 2006), and Dora Apel and Shawn Michelle Smith, *Lynching Photographs* (Berkeley: University of California Press, 2008).

80. Martinez, *Injustice Never Leaves You,* 232.

81. Carrigan and Webb, *Forgotten Dead,* 9–10.

of social authority on the individual, at the same time that it connects the individual to a larger community of fellow witnesses."[82] To witness a lynching was also a deeply embodied and sensory-laden practice. Witnessing an execution included "being physically near the scene of the action and among a crowd of like-minded people. To witness a hanging was also to hear the proceedings and perhaps the cries of the condemned, and to feel the push of the crowd, to sense that one was a part of something important or extraordinary." For Wood, understanding the power of lynchings requires making sense of the sensorium of *pleasure* that so many white southerners inhabited when witnessing racial violence.[83]

Race riots, lynch mobs, and various forms of vigilante violence that included the burning, shooting, drowning, and stabbing of Mexican and other nonwhite subjects are all examples of white citizens having access to a democratic, rights-based political system characterized by equality and the rule of law *for them,* alongside the opportunity to both witness and exercise arbitrary authority over various racial populations—up to and including the freedom to partake in melodramatic spectacles of mass violence. For certain white citizens, the opportunity to be the bearer of rights and legal equality while being free to deny those same rights to racialized communities was an intoxicating civic synthesis.

82. Wood, *Lynching and Spectacle,* 4.
83. Wood, 31, 24.

3. Authorized Violence: Migrant Suffering and Participatory (White) Democracy

IN TODAY'S UNITED STATES, white citizens no longer enjoy the pleasure of having access to a state, and state institutions, *explicitly* committed to whiteness as standing through statute and even constitutional sanction.[1] Yet today, white advantage operates as a form of *social* power, as a system of tacit racial privileges reproduced through economic inequality, the racial wealth gap, and everyday practices that presume white advantage.[2] Moreover, as philosopher Linda Martín Alcoff has observed, whether acknowledged or not, whiteness is "a prominent feature of one's way of being in the world," affecting "how one navigates the world, and of how one is navigated around by others."[3]

Today, for citizens who remain invested in whiteness as "a badge of status," there are fewer and fewer legally sanctioned outlets for publicly engaging in Herrenvolk practices. And it's my contention that this is a key reason that public proclamations regarding the policing and punishing of migrants have emerged as such an affectively charged practice for nativists. Anti-migrant rhetoric alongside acts of noncitizen violence offers nativists democratic pleasures that are increasingly difficult to access in the post-Herrenvolk era. Providing an outlet and legally sanctioned target for their rage and fear, anti-migrant violence represents a kind of

1. Olson, "Whiteness and the Polarization of American Politics," 709.
2. Olson.
3. Alcoff, *Future of Whiteness*, 9.

Herrenvolk loophole, granting white citizens access to one of the few racialized populations that can still be made legally subject to the violent rhetoric and practices of white democracy. Today, the legacy of anti-Mexican violence, the dehumanizing rhetoric, and migrants' ongoing criminalization—alongside their status as noncitizens—are what make the "Mexican illegal" such a potent subject for the white nativist imaginary. Classified as both illegal and criminal, unauthorized migrants are particularly vulnerable to both state-sanctioned and extralegal practices of violence, enforcement, terror, exclusion, and removal.

Beyond watching television and consuming print media, for those thinking about going beyond being spectators to anti-migrant violence, there is also a significant anti-immigrant public sphere. Created through social media, participating in an alternative public sphere includes posting on Twitter, Instagram, and Facebook as well as reading and posting to online message board on sites such as 8kun.[4] For those more inclined to get their hands dirty, participating in immigration enforcement gives both regular citizens and agents of the state the right to invoke the rule of law to exert domination over the movement and placement of nonwhite bodies. Moreover, because migrants are often depicted as *choosing* to move and enter the country illegally, enforcement and sanctions are authorized through the discursive terrain of liberalism and the rule of law. Unlike other Herrenvolk practices that are now legally prohibited, aggressive immigration enforcement can be witnessed and enacted by a liberal polity whose citizens and policing apparatus can legitimately claim that its actions have been democratically approved as lawful, necessary, and authorized.

4. 8kun is the rebranded, relaunched message board formerly known as 8chan, which went offline in August 2019 after white supremacist content was linked to multiple mass shootings. 8chan itself was an offshoot of 4chan, a less controversial message board that still operates.

Militia Groups

With the U.S.-Mexican border continuing to serve as "a hive for policing," nativists have a variety of opportunities to engage in both paid and unpaid practices of migrant violence. For those in search of meaning and community, right-wing paramilitary groups operating along the U.S.–Mexican border offer nativists the opportunity to reenact particular forms of frontier freedom—engaging in vigilante violence and policing migrants as way to wield, protect, and exceed the law, saving the region from "invasion" and misrule. Moreover, as Harel Shapira observes in his ethnography of the Minutemen Civil Defense Corps, many militia members are older male veterans, divorced and anxious about their own status. Nostalgic for the past and afraid of a future in which they don't clearly see themselves, members of the militia movement are engaged in what Shapira calls "a project of the self."[5] For these (mostly) men, participating in a militia represents a democratic, embodied, and participatory space where members get to use equipment, carry guns, sleep in tents, patrol the border, and stand guard. Turning to the militia to "extend their tour of duty" by policing the U.S.–Mexican border, militia members have an opportunity to revisit and reenact their military past.[6]

According to Shapira, militia men often use the border as "a resource for restoring conditions of life that they have struggled to maintain: soldiering, securing the nation, protecting family members, and establishing masculine camaraderie."[7] Yet, in seeking to understand his subjects, Shapira seeks to redeem them, defending them as "civic-minded actors" in search of meaning and encouraging his readers to avoid "tired accounts of racism."[8] But

5. Harel Shapira, *Waiting for José: The Minutemen's Pursuit of America* (Princeton, N.J.: Princeton University Press, 2013), 22, 36.

6. Shapira, 25.

7. Shapira, 152.

8. Shapira, 20.

in creating this binary between actors who are racist and those who are civic-minded, Shapira's analysis exposes why so many liberal thinkers struggle to theorize whiteness in relation to our understanding of democracy, freedom, and citizenship. Because categories such as democracy, citizenship, and freedom are self-evidently good, racism must be *separate* from what makes the Minutemen a civic organization. Yet, seen through the prism of Herrenvolk democracy, anti-migrant violence appears not as the antithesis of these civic values and practices but merely as one troubling form of their enactment.

Militia groups exemplify how members' right to patrol the border, arresting and detaining migrants, serves as a kind of proxy for liberation, a return to a form of frontier freedom premised on a belief that freedom is the ability to move freely across the landscape, engaging in practices of terror and removal that are both legal and extrajudicial. Here the "regenerative power of the frontier" is briefly resuscitated when groups participate with their fellow militia members in pursuing, policing, threatening, and/or apprehending Mexicans. In this instance, movement emerges as a "technology of citizenship," where the movement of certain subjects is deemed free and desirable, while the movement of others is considered excessive and subject to punishment and regulation.[9] A recent example of this dynamic happened in April 2019, when the United Constitutional Patriots detained three hundred Central Americans seeking asylum, including children.[10] An armed civilian militia comprising veterans and former police officers who patrol the border to "uphold and defend the Constitution of the United States," the United Constitutional Patriots have posted online dozens of videos of their group patrolling and detaining migrants they found in the desert.[11] In the case of the three hundred asylum

9. Kotef, "Violent Attachments," 15.

10. Aaron Martinez, "Armed Civilians Are Detaining Migrants at the Border. The ACLU Wants Them Investigated," *El Paso Times*, April 19, 2019.

11. Martinez.

seekers, the group livestreamed the arrest on Facebook, showing the detained migrants alongside the presence of the Border Patrol (who were called to the scene and who took the migrant families into custody) and a voice-over repeatedly intoning, "This is an invasion—and it is never, never ending."[12] Like the images of civilians and U.S. soldiers posing with Texas Rangers in photos of Mexicans lined up prior to (and following) execution, the Facebook videos of militia members with detained migrants and Border Patrol agents parallel the long history of local authorities and deputized citizens coming together in conspicuous acts of violence against Mexicans. And like the earlier use of photographs, today's social media posts help sustain the profoundly *public* character of such violence against migrants.

La Migra: Immigration and Customs Enforcement and Border Patrol

Beyond volunteerism, citizens revisit practices of whiteness and racialized standing through their participation in the activities of Immigration and Customs Enforcement (ICE) and the U.S. Customs and Border Protection (CBP). The enforcement mandate involved in working for ICE or CBP authorizes the apprehending, processing, detaining, and deporting of "illegal and criminal aliens."[13] Agents are responsible for detecting, preventing, and apprehending migrants—a process that includes conducting raids, surveilling, tracking migrants, and utilizing various forms of technology and military equipment to engage in enforcement both at the border and in the nation's interior.

12. Martinez; Alicia A. Caldwell, "Civilian Militia Group Stops Migrants at the U.S.–Mexico Border," *Wall Street Journal*, April 19, 2019.

13. Hernández, *Migra!*; Todd Miller, *Border Patrol Nation: Dispatches from the Front Lines of Homeland Security* (San Francisco: City Lights, 2014); Francisco Cantú, *The Line Becomes a River* (New York: Riverhead, 2018); Jason de León, *The Land of Open Graves: Living and Dying on the Migrant Trail* (Berkeley: University of California Press, 2015).

And while many agency employees are surely *not* nativists or driven by racist inclinations, the very enforcement mandates of both federal agencies are shaped by policing logics that include violent and racially discriminatory origin stories regarding the culture of policing in the United States.[14] For example, as Kelly Lytle Hernández has written in her history of the Border Patrol, at its inception in 1924, the agency absorbed a substantial number of former Texas Rangers who brought their anti-Mexican racism and violence to the federal level. As Hernández notes, the majority of this first generation of border agents were working-class Anglo men who had grown up witnessing violence against Mexicans. These men saw law enforcement "as a strategy of economic survival and social uplift in the agricultural-based societies of the borderlands."[15] Empowered by the state to enforce the law, here we can see how Border Patrol agents were given the "wages of whiteness."[16] Agents sought to gain their own dignity and status through enacting violence against Mexicans: by claiming "whiteness, manhood, and respect," agents were rewarded with "public, psychological, and material" resources.[17]

Given the Border Patrol's origins, it's no surprise that Latinos were initially a tiny minority of its force. But the agency has long actively recruited Spanish-speaking employees. By 1989, Latinos made up more than one-third of the agency; today, more than 50 percent of Border Patrol agents and 24 percent of ICE agents are Latinx.[18] With

14. Will Carless and Michael Corey, "To Protect and Slur: Inside Hate Groups on Facebook, Police Officers Trade Racist Memes, Conspiracy Theories and Islamophobia," *Reveal,* June 14, 2019; Michelle Alexander, *The New Jim Crow: Mass Incarceration in the Age of Colorblindness* (New York: New Press, 2012); Andrew Dilts, *Punishment and Inclusion: Race, Membership, and the Limits of American Liberalism* (New York: Fordham University Press, 2014); Angela Davis, *Are Prisons Obsolete?* (New York: Seven Stories Press, 2003).

15. Hernández, *Migra!,* 20–23.

16. David Roediger, xx.

17. Hernández, *Migra!,* 55.

18. See David Cortez, "I Asked Why They Joined Immigration Law

high unemployment in rural border areas, the Border Patrol is often a top local employer, promising government jobs with good benefits and job security. In a neoliberal economy characterized by austerity and a shrinking social welfare base, homeland security has emerged as a growing site of state-subsidized employment.[19] As Todd Miller has written, the border is both a region and a growth industry with a "border–industrial complex" characterized by jobs, industries, and revenue.[20] Moreover, the Border Patrol represents one of the remaining well-paid jobs that doesn't require a bachelor's degree.[21] With some agents starting at $49,000 plus benefits, CBP promises officers entry into the middle class.[22] As one Latino agent in Texas observed, "here in Imperial Valley," with an agent's salary, "you'll be upper middle-class."[23] In his interviews with Latinos working in immigration enforcement, political scientist David Cortez found that while some Latinx agents felt bad about working immigration and expressed misgivings about the job, they also expressed a

---

Enforcement. Now I'm Urging Them to Leave," *USA Today,* July 3, 2019, and Brittny Mejia, "Many Latinos Answer Call of the Border Patrol in the Age of Trump," *Los Angeles Times,* April 12, 2018.

19. Cortez, "I Asked Why They Joined Immigration Law Enforcement."

20. As Monica Muñoz Martinez notes, in 2015, the United States spent nearly $2 billion on immigration detention centers. Martinez, *Injustice Never Leaves You,* 296. With multiple economic incentives to militarize the border, the United States now spends more on the "border–industrial complex" than it spends on the Federal Bureau of Investigation and the Drug Enforcement Agency combined. See Todd Miller, *Border Patrol Nation: Dispatches from the Front Lines of Homeland Security* (San Francisco: City Lights, 2014). As Martinez notes, since 2009, "congressional appropriation laws have included language that sets a quota to maintain 34,000 immigration detention beds on a daily basis. US Immigration and Customs Enforcement [ICE] is the only law enforcement agency subject to a statutory quota." Martinez, *Injustice Never Leaves You,* 296.

21. Esther Cepeda, "Don't Judge Latinos Who Patrol the Border until You Walk in Their Shoes," *Al Día,* May 2, 2018.

22. Rory Carroll, "Life as a Mexican American on the Border Patrol: 'The System Is Not Broken,'" *Guardian,* December 12, 2016.

23. Mejia, "Many Latinos Answer Call."

willingness to do whatever they had to do to protect and provide for their families. In expressing ambivalence about engaging in actions they would prefer not to undertake, Cortez remarks, "It is tough to ignore the parallels between statements like these and those of migrants willing to risk their lives and flout immigration laws in the hopes of providing a better life for their families here in the United States."[24] Here we see how limited opportunity and economic precarity are coercive forces pushing both Latinx agents and migrants toward undesirable labor and practices of survival that are sometimes judged by others as unacceptable and criminal.

Latinx agents both complicate and reinforce the politics of whiteness and Herrenvolk democracy. As noted earlier, because Latinos "have no simple positioning in the U.S. racial order," their proximity to whiteness alongside their racial indeterminacy makes assaults on migrants and Latinx populations both *more* feasible and defensible.[25] Together, both Latinx and non-Latinx CBP and ICE agents are free to partake in racist and dehumanizing speech and acts against "illegals," shielded by a color-blind discourse defined in terms of criminality, sovereignty, legality, and fairness. Latinos' simultaneous presence as both police and population legitimates Herrenvolk violence, justifying and obscuring the supremacist logics at play.

Despite being part of a multiracial organization, Border Patrol agents have been criticized for abusing and mistreating migrant men, women, and children in custody and while apprehending them. In *The Line Becomes a River,* Francisco Cantú, a former agent who is Mexican American, describes the pervasive culture of casual racism and destruction in which officers participate, including destroying water and food caches out in the field, ripping up and scattering the clothes found in migrants' backpacks, and

24. Cortez, "I Asked Why They Joined Immigration Law Enforcement."

25. See Bebout, *Whiteness on the Border,* 4; see also Gomez, *Manifest Destinies*; Hattam, *In the Shadow of Race*; Mora, *Making Hispanics.*

laughing while urinating on migrants' ransacked belongings.[26] Noting that many agents are former cops, ex-soldiers, and folks tired of low-wage jobs and limited opportunities, Cantú describes agents as being trained to see the border as a war zone of cartels and narcotraffickers—when in fact what agents mostly encounter are human beings fleeing poverty and violence. Cantú notes that agents often refer to such migrants as POWs, short for "plain old wets."[27]

In 2019, ProPublica exposed a secret Facebook group for current and former Border Patrol agents, a forum for some ninety-five hundred members who shared sexist memes, made xenophobic comments, and poked fun at migrant deaths. The group, called "I'm 10–15" (CBP code for "aliens in custody"), described itself as a forum for both "funny" and "serious" discussion about Border Patrol work, stating in its introduction, "Remember you are never alone in this family."[28] Discussing an upcoming visit to two Texas stations by members of the Congressional Hispanic Caucus and their Democratic colleagues, members of the Facebook group encouraged agents to hurl a "burrito at these bitches" and posted a vulgar illustration depicting Representative Alexandria Ocasio-Cortez "engaged in oral sex with a detained migrant."[29] Another, apparently a patrol supervisor, wrote, "Fuck the hoes."[30]

Commenting on a photo of Salvadoran migrant Óscar Alberto Martínez Ramírez and his twenty-three-month-old daughter

26. Cantú, *Line Becomes a River,* 20, 33, 28.
27. Cantú, 101.
28. A. C. Thompson, "Inside the Secret Border Patrol Facebook Group Where Agents Joke about Migrant Deaths and Post Sexist Memes," *ProPublica,* July 1, 2019. After a yearlong investigation, CBP fired four agents and suspended thirty-eight without pay; see Molly O'Toole, "Border Agency Fires 4 for Secret Facebook Groups with Violent, Bigoted Posts," *Los Angeles Times,* July 16, 2020.
29. Thompson, "Inside the Secret Border Patrol Facebook Group."
30. Thompson.

Valeria's lifeless bodies lying face down in the Rio Grande,[31] a poster called them "floaters" and wondered if their bodies were photoshopped by "liberals," because they look "too clean."[32] The photo, and the conspiratorial description, echoes Monica Muñoz Martinez's earlier discussion of how postcards of Mexican corpses in the early twentieth century were circulated as "a bonding mechanism for those who shared the images," serving as "a continued method of racial intimidation."[33]

The "I'm 10–15" Facebook group also highlights the misogyny that has long plagued the agency. As the Southern Border Communities Coalition has noted, the Border Patrol has the lowest percentage of female agents or officers in any federal law enforcement agency. Such displays of racism and sexism within the agency are also a reminder that Herrenvolk logics are always informed by questions of gender and sexuality. Perhaps agents manage racial difference within the Border Patrol through their shared desire to celebrate acts of misogyny and heteronormative violence, creating community through a culture of cruelty aimed at migrants, sexual minorities, and women.

While there is no breakdown of the racial makeup of the "I'm 10–15" Facebook page, the ongoing Herrenvolk logics of the Border Patrol remind us that whiteness is "a *political* color," one that distinguishes "the free from the unfree, the equal from the inferior, the citizen from the slave."[34] I would supplement this claim to explore how the political color of whiteness also distinguishes citizen from noncitizen. For while an earlier form of Herrenvolk democracy allowed white citizens to rule themselves democratically "while imposing tyranny over a nonwhite majority," today nativists use the category *citizen* to create a new version of white-

31. Thompson.

32. HipLatina, "Why So Many Latino Men Join the Border Patrol That Dehumanizes Latinos," July 2, 2019.

33. Martinez, *Injustice Never Leaves You,* 232.

34. Olson, *Abolition of White Democracy,* 43.

ness as standing.[35] Moreover, with white citizens more ideologically divided over their own relationship to whiteness, today it is migrants—noncitizens—who provide "the glass floor below which the white citizen could see but never fall." Paraphrasing Olson, today's version of whiteness as standing insists that "no matter how poor, mean, or ignorant one might have been, or whatever discrimination on the basis of gender, class, religion, or ethnicity one may have been subjected to, one could always derive social esteem (and often draw on public resources) by asserting, 'At least I'm not undocumented.'"[36] Like African Americans in the Herrenvolk era, migrants are not simply noncitizens but *anticitizens.* Not merely excluded from the social compact, migrants are "the Other that simultaneously threatened and consolidated it."[37]

In recent years, the Border Patrol has expanded dramatically, with dangerous results. When the agency added eight thousand officers between 2006 and 2009, for example, the number of employees arrested for misconduct (civil rights violations or off-duty crimes, such as domestic violence) increased by 44 percent during the three-year span.[38] More recently, in an effort by the Trump administration to hire fifteen thousand new Border Patrol and ICE agents, the Department of Homeland Security in 2017 moved to ease training and enrollment requirements for Border Patrol agents, removing things such as "language proficiency tests" and some of the physical fitness tests in order to speed up hiring.[39] Such hiring practices will only increase the chances that undertrained ICE and Border Patrol agents will impose tyrannical rule over nonwhite majorities, discovering and creating innumerable opportunities to both wield and exceed the law. Moreover, a lack

35. Van den Berghe, *Race and Racism,* 101.

36. Olson, "Whiteness and the Polarization of American Politics," 708; see also Olson, *Abolition of White Democracy,* 43.

37. Olson, *Abolition of White Democracy,* 43.

38. Martinez, *Injustice Never Leaves You,* 297.

39. Martinez, 297–98.

of education and training will make it easier to produce agents comfortable moving between the legal and extralegal—violating human rights law and making them complicit in practices long deemed inhumane.

ICE leaders are increasingly ordering agents to conduct mass raids with the goal of indiscriminately rounding up, detaining, and deporting migrants, a practice that terrorizes communities while tearing apart families.[40] ICE agents are obeying orders to separate children from their parents, confine children to cages, force adults into overcrowded pens, and deny migrants adequate food and water, or even soap, showers, and toothbrushes.[41] Military officers have tasked soldiers with putting up lethal concertina wire on fencing near border towns, creating a permanent potential for harm to any human or animal who goes near the wire.[42] In a recent example of state agents both wielding and exceeding the law, Border Patrol officers—who do *not* have the authority to evaluate the validity of asylum claims—have falsified documents and lied to migrants seeking asylum so that they would return (or be returned) to their home countries.[43]

Like soldiers during the Mexican-American War, ICE and Border Patrol agents acting with minimal training and supervision inside a massive and decentralized homeland security state can easily come to see the violence they commit as a form of liberty, for both the nation and themselves.[44] Indeed, when it comes to

40. Sophia Tesfaye, "The Truth about Trump's ICE Raids: Botched Mississippi Operation Is Good Optics," *Salon*, August 9, 2019.

41. Meagan Flynn, "Detained Migrant Children Got No Toothbrush, No Soap, No Sleep. It's No Problem, Government Argues," *Washington Post*, June 21, 2019.

42. Rebecca Onion, "That Beautiful Barbed: The Concertina Wire Trump Loves at the Border Has a Long, Troubling Legacy in the West," *Slate*, November 6, 2018.

43. Cora Currier, "Emboldened by Trump, U.S. Border Officials Are Lying to Asylum Seekers and Turning Them Away," *Intercept*, July 12, 2017.

44. Grandin, *End of the Myth*, 98.

the politics of immigration, the "rule of law" has a very specific meaning—it refers to using state and citizen power in the service of domination. Law is police (Border and ICE agents), not judges. In the logic of Herrenvolk democracy, law, not the courts, sanctions force. Indeed, this is why Trump and his nativist supporters can continually extol the rule of law while disparaging judges and opposing the hiring of immigration judges to process asylum claims. Nativists don't want judges and courts to create more efficient rules to manage movement—instead, they want to enhance punishment. This is why, for nativists, an independent and bipartisan judiciary is seen as thwarting the rule of law, paradoxical as that may sound.[45] For example, when a federal judge in Seattle blocked a Trump administration order allowing for the indefinite detention of some asylum seekers, the White House claimed that the ruling was "at war with the rule of law."[46] This is why when judges (even those appointed by Republicans) refuse to grant the right to exclude or sanction racially infused acts of suffering or violence, Trump characterizes them as "biased," "horrible," or "a disgrace."[47] When nativists say "we are losing our country" and "if we don't have laws, we don't have a country," the loss being articulated is that if the government doesn't allow white citizens some capacity to inflict racialized violence with relative impunity, the United States will no longer *be* a white democracy. For Trump and his nativist supporters, the law is supposed to be Herrenvolk law, helping to explain why Trump blames "Obama judges" for unfavorable decisions, while rarely if ever referring to justices as "Carter" or "Clinton" judges; the racism is implicit but undeniable. This also explains why nativists can so easily label as

45. Brennan Center for Justice, "In His Own Words: The President's Attacks on the Courts," June 5, 2017.

46. Jacqueline Thomsen, "White House Says Judge Blocking Order on Asylum-Seekers 'at War' with Rule of Law," *Hill,* July 3, 2019.

47. Adam Liptak, "Trump Takes Aim at Appeals Court, Calling It a 'Disgrace,'" *New York Times,* November 20, 2018.

"biased" nonwhite judges, such as Gonzalo Curiel, who presided over the Trump University case.[48] For nativists, an investment in white democracy is the precondition for legitimacy.

For citizens who long to revisit the politics of whiteness as standing, the practices of ICE and CBP offer the right to use the law to police other populations, to impose tyranny while participating in forms of violence that feel like freedom—economic freedom, the freedom to enforce the law, and the frontier freedom of engaging in practices of settler sovereignty characterized by forced removal and transfer. For those enamored of whiteness as standing, power also lies in *spectacles* of racialized violence and cruelty. Granted, today a majority of Americans are appalled by pictures of children in cages, migrants falling sick with coronavirus at detention centers, families running from tear gas at the border, parents and children crying at being separated, ICE agents arresting migrants at their homes and workplaces, and newspaper and TV accounts of the filth and stench experienced by migrants in overcrowded holding pens. But these accounts—including quotes from horrified pro-immigrant advocates—offer nativists a particular form of pleasure, a "vicarious spectacle" of violence that satisfies their longing to see the United States defending its sovereignty. Such depictions of migrant violence assure nativists that those in charge are finally "defending our borders" and "doing something" about the scourge of illegal immigration.[49]

Beyond visual spectacles of cruelty, in the case of immigration, the Trump administration has filled key offices with aggressively nativist staffers bent on implementing changes in immigration policy that would sharply restrict not only illegal immigration but *legal* immigration, particularly from Latin America, Africa, and parts of Asia. Individuals like Stephen Miller, Jeff Sessions, and John Kelly have all been part of a large and sustained effort

48. Brent Kendall, "Trump Says Judge's Mexican Heritage Presents 'Absolute Conflicts,'" *Wall Street Journal*, June 3, 2016.

49. Wood, *Lynching and Spectacle*, 28.

not only to characterize the current migrant population as a racialized threat—invasive, dishonest, destructive, dependent, and criminal—but to transform rhetoric into major changes in immigration policy.[50]

The Trump Rally

Beyond spectacles of violence and changes in policy, nativists in the Trump era have access to the democratic and participatory experience of the "Make America Great Again" (MAGA) rally. Along with anti-Muslim screeds and attacks on Black-run cities, MAGA rallies offer participants the opportunity to revisit a colonial and frontier imaginary defined by anti-Mexican and anti-Indian violence—conjuring an anti-Latinx dystopia populated by invasive caravans from Central America, MS-13 gang members, rapists, and criminals. Trump rallies often feature him telling stories of undocumented migrants arrested locally and bringing onstage the relatives of people killed by undocumented immigrants (a group he calls "angel families") to highlight their suffering and justify his restrictive immigration proposals.[51] Like nineteenth-century

50. Nick Miroff and Josh Dawsey, "The Adviser Who Scripts Trump's Immigration Policy," *Washington Post,* August 17, 2019; Jason DeParle, "How Stephen Miller Seized the Moment to Battle Immigration," *New York Times,* August 17, 2019; Catherine Rampell, "Trump's Immigration Policies Speak Louder than His Racist, Xenophobic Words," *Washington Post,* July 18, 2019; Catherine Rampell, "The 1930s Were a Dark Period for Immigration Policies. There's One Way Today's Could Be Worse," *Washington Post,* July 22, 2019; Molly O'Toole, "Trump Moves to Eliminate Nearly All Asylum Claims at Southern Border," *Los Angeles Times,* July 15, 2019; Michael D. Shear, Miriam Jordan, and Caitlin Dickerson, "Trump's Policy Could Alter the Face of the American Immigrant," *New York Times,* August 14, 2019.

51. During his campaign rallies, Trump often gave melodramatic accounts of young American women murdered by "criminal aliens" living illegally in the United States. On the presidential campaign trail, Trump repeatedly referred to the killing of Kate Steinle in San Francisco. Speaking to Anderson Cooper about Steinle in July 2015, Trump stated, "This man, or this animal, that shot that wonderful, that beautiful woman in San

newspaper accounts that sought to satisfy white readers with the "excruciating details" of lynchings, Trump's rally speeches conjure images of "deadly sanctuary cities" where "dangerous, violent, criminal aliens" are continually "hacking and raping and bludgeoning" American citizens.[52] As with earlier visions of *los indios bárbaros,* migrants are depicted as both lawless and monstrous, subjects who "roam," "raid," and kill without mercy—a population who must be "excised not simply from the geographical borders of nation, but from the very boundaries of humanity."[53]

In the face of such looming depravity, rallygoers can take solace in their shared fear and outrage regarding what they see as an existential threat facing the United States. At the same time, beyond their anger and fear, attendees can also take pleasure in the wild freedom and impunity of Trump's violent rhetoric. Witnessing each other cheering for a world of racialized violence and removal, rallygoers are encouraged to imagine a society in which migrants can be treated with impunity—rounded up, arrested, punished, and deported at will. Galvanized by the president's Twitter feed and the amplification of his messages on Fox News, Trump rallies offer nativists access to a collective space of community—one in which supporters can gather together in public, delight in the crowd, and

---

Francisco, this guy was pushed back by Mexico. . . . Mexico pushes back people across the border that are criminals, that are drug dealers." Indeed, a few weeks into his presidency, Trump signed one of his first executive orders, creating the Victims of Immigration Crime Engagement (VOICE), an office within ICE for which "angel families" had advocated despite the fact that immigrants (including the undocumented) commit fewer crimes than native-born citizens. See Dave Mosher, "Mollie Tibbetts' Death Is Being Used to Push Debunked Ideas about Illegal Immigration and Violent Crime," *Business Insider,* August 22, 2018; Kenneth P. Vogel and Katie Rogers, "For Trump and 'Angel Families,' a Mutually Beneficial Bond," *New York Times,* July 4, 2018.

52. Jeff Sharlet, "He's the Chosen One to Run America: Inside the Cult of Trump, His Rallies Are Church and He Is the Gospel," *Vanity Fair,* June 18, 2020.

53. Saldaña-Portillo, *Indian Given,* 257.

share in the scandalous thrill of Trump's outrageous and racially inflammatory speech. Wearing hats and T-shirts bearing violent, misogynistic, and/or racist phrases, slogan-chanting supporters get a chance to experience elements of white mob violence by publicly indulging their desire for freedom from restraint.[54] Like spectators at a lynching, Trump rallies bring the attendees together in a shared act of witnessing.[55] Gathering to behold an American president using extreme and often racist language to enact "a drama of retribution against sin and criminality," rallygoers join together in a vicarious spectacle of violence, chanting phrases like "build the wall," "lock her up," and "send them back," while booing press photographers and reporters. Experiencing the "push of the crowd" while being "physically near the scene of the action and among a crowd of like-minded people," spectators at a Trump rally are united through a shared sensorium and in the belief that they are witness to something "important or extraordinary."[56] Through rituals of participation and performance, MAGA rally attendees get to revisit elements of white democracy to which citizens had access in the Herrenvolk era.[57]

54. Speaking at a rally in Florida in May, Trump asked his audience how to stop migrants from crossing into the United States. When a woman at the rally shouted "shoot them!" Trump only smiled, saying, "Only in the Panhandle can you get away with that statement." Three months later, in El Paso, Texas, the United States experienced one of the deadliest hate crimes ever committed against Latinos. See Paloma Esquivel, Esmeralda Bermudez, Giulia McConnell Nieto Del Rio, Louis Sahagun, and Cindy Carcamo, "For Latinos, El Paso Is a Devastating New Low in a Trump Era," *San Diego Union-Tribune,* August 5, 2019; J. M. Rieger, "When a Rallygoer Suggested Shooting Immigrants in May, Trump Made a Joke," *Washington Post,* August 5, 2019.

55. Wood, *Lynching and Spectacle,* 40.

56. Wood, 31.

57. Felicia Sonmez and Mike DeBonis, "Trump Tells Four Liberal Congresswomen to 'Go Back' to Their Countries, Prompting Pelosi to Defend Them," *Washington Post,* July 14, 2019; Brett Samuels, "Trump Rally Crowd Chants 'Send Her Back' about Ilhan Omar," *Hill,* July 17, 2019.

At the same time, as our earlier discussion of Latinx border agents has shown (and as scholars of race have long noted), "the form of white supremacy peculiar to the United States is oriented not simply toward a commitment to racial purity" but toward a multiracial vision of a nation premised on "racial hierarchy and white domination."[58] From performances of blackface minstrelsy to Mexican-themed attractions, to acts of exoticization and demonization of the Chinese and other Asian populations, to practices of "playing Indian" that mythologized Indigenous people while also supporting practices of settler colonialism—in the United States, a relationship of "love and theft" alongside a logic of multiculturalism serves to reproduce white nationalism.[59] African American conservatives such as Lynnette Hardaway and Rochelle Richardson (better known as the duo Diamond and Silk) are just one vivid example of such right-wing multiculturalism. Deploying their racial and gender identities in the service of anti-migrant violence and race-conscious xenophobic nationalism, Diamond and Silk speak as Black women against the way African Americans have been unfairly criminalized. Contrasting these unfair anti-Black attitudes to the "real criminality" of the undocumented, Diamond and Silk declare that "if Bill Clinton can do mass incarceration . . . we can do mass deportation."[60]

Even more meaningful for our purposes, Trump rallies are also made more diverse by the presence of *Latino* Trump support-

58. HoSang and Lowndes, *Producers, Parasites, Patriots,* 104.

59. HoSang and Lowndes, 109; see also Eric Lott, *Love and Theft: Blackface Minstrelsy and the American Working Class* (New York: Oxford University Press, 1993); Cecilia Márquez, "Becoming Pedro: 'Playing Mexican' at South of the Border," *Latino Studies* 16, no. 4 (2018): 461–81; John Kuo Wei Tchen, *New York before Chinatown: Orientalism and the Shaping of American Culture, 1776–1882* (Baltimore: Johns Hopkins University Press, 2001); Philip J. Deloria, *Playing Indian* (New Haven, Conn.: Yale University Press, 1999); Richard Slotkin, *Regeneration through Violence: The Mythology of the American Frontier* (Norman: University of Oklahoma Press, 1973); Rogin, *Fathers and Children.*

60. HoSang and Lowndes, *Producers, Parasites, Patriots,* 112.

ers, a group that appears to many an inexplicable segment of the Republican Party's electorate. In *The Hispanic Republican,* historian Geraldo Cadava confronts this riddle head-on, asking, "Why have Hispanics continued to support the Republican Party, even Trump's Republican Party?" Noting that Trump received almost 30 percent of the Latino vote in 2016, Cadava asks, "How has the Republican Party built a Hispanic base to withstand attacks by leaders who devalue them?"[61] To answer these questions, Cadava embarks on a history of Hispanic Republican elites and their participation in the GOP over the past half-century. While Trump has been a polarizing figure "for Hispanic Republicans . . . he hasn't turned many of them away."[62] Writing before the global COVID-19 pandemic devastated the U.S. economy, Cadava describes Trump's Hispanic supporters as pleased with the president's tax cuts, America's low unemployment rate, the fact that financial regulations have been slashed, and efforts to protect the United States from the threat of Venezuela-style socialism.[63] Pointing to the millions of dollars the Republican National Committee has spent on grassroots Hispanic outreach, Cadava quotes a Hispanic Republican asserting that "whatever Trump said about immigrants and border walls," Hispanics were convinced that "the Republican Party would put them to work and help them buy homes." Noting that "most of Trump's Hispanic supporters don't believe that Trump is racist," Cadava concludes his analysis by arguing that while "Hispanic Republicans would, of course, prefer that their party be more inclusive," there are multiple reasons "why Republican candidates still win a significant share of Hispanic votes, even if Hispanic voters disagree with a particular candidate's positions or style."[64]

61. Geraldo Cadava, *The Hispanic Republican: The Shaping of an American Political Identity, from Nixon to Trump* (New York: HarperCollins, 2020), xii–xiii.

62. Cadava, 335, 336.

63. Cadava, xii.

64. Cadava, 337.

Cadava's account of Hispanic Republicans is enormously helpful in showing readers the history of Hispanic GOP elites and how they organized to make a space for themselves in the Republican Party. But this analysis conflates these elites, often from older generations, with rank-and-file Latino voters currently supporting Trump and the GOP. However, what Cadava's analysis fails to consider, what he averts his eyes from, is the possibility that many Latinx supporters of Trump may actually approve of and take pleasure in Trump's MAGA rallies and in his most undemocratic, outrageous, or violent assertions—even when that violence targets migrants and other people of color. This segment of the electorate may be animated by anti-Black racism. They may feel little or no connection to recent immigrants, particularly the undocumented.[65] They may view migrants as racially Other, as welfare cheats or dangerous lawbreakers. Perhaps they don't share Trump's hostility toward migrants—but they *do* share his hatred of Obama and suspicion of the "deep state." Perhaps they delight in Trump's misogyny, his Islamophobia, his celebrations of police power, or his attacks on science and media.

As noted earlier, because Latinos "have no simple positioning in the U.S. racial order," they too are capable of becoming "agents in the reproduction of racial subordination" even as they are victims of it. Embracing the politics of white democracy in an effort to secure their own rights and privileges, Latino Trump supporters may not only tolerate the party's embrace of Herrenvolk democracy—they may welcome it.

65. Jennifer Medina, "Most Latinos Don't Back Trump. But Some Wear Their Support Proudly," *New York Times*, September 18, 2019.

Conclusion: Migrant Futurity, Divided Whiteness, and the Authoritarian Turn

AS I HAVE ARGUED, violence against migrants creates a kind of Herrenvolk *loophole* for nativists—offering them a legally sanctioned opportunity to impose tyranny over a nonwhite population while still claiming constitutional protections for themselves. Yet despite the damage it does to migrants and our democratic values more broadly, it's also my contention that anti-migrant violence ultimately *fails* to satisfy the desire for whiteness as standing. Because today, whiteness no longer possesses the same economic and political guarantees it once did. Indeed, many white citizens (particularly older conservatives) are melancholic over what they perceive as an increasingly dismal and limited future. Once able to contrast their own standing against nonwhite populations (including the collective right to legally enforce segregated spaces and institutions), today, whiteness is not only a less public and participatory practice but also a privilege that occurs at a more aggregate level.[1] Despite the fact that whites as a group "are statistically much more likely to go to college, buy a house, and be gainfully employed," there is no guarantee that any individual white person will personally benefit.[2] So while nonwhite populations still experience racial profiling, police violence, redlining, educational inequalities, dramatically higher levels of incarceration, and other race-based disadvantages, today's white advantage involves "probabilities, not guarantees."[3] Interestingly, as Olson

1. Olson, "Whiteness and the Polarization of American Politics," 709.
2. Olson, 709.
3. Olson, *Abolition of White Democracy*, 76.

observed, the troubling paradox inherent in the recent shift from white *standing* to white *normalization* is that it "perpetuates white advantage while also creating new forms of white insecurity and resentment because such benefits are less certain."[4]

Making the racial situation more fraught, this growing sense of white precarity is occurring in the context of four decades of privatization, deregulation, and regressive tax policy. As numerous scholars have noted, the United States has been undergoing the most massive upward transfer of wealth it has experienced since the Gilded Age of the late nineteenth century.[5] Today, more people are working longer hours for less and less and have seen state support in the form of social services evaporate[6]—a gap that turned into an economic abyss as soon as the COVID-19 pandemic shutdown put pressure on low-wage "essential workers," hospitals, unemployment-insurance systems, and social infrastructure.[7] Sustained political attacks have dramatically weakened institutions that traditionally protect the middle and working classes: labor unions, progressive income and wealth taxation policies, social welfare programs, consumer protections, and civil rights and antidiscrimination laws. Finally, changes in immigration policy (such as the 1965 Immigration and Nationality Act) eliminated the use of national-origin quotas, moving U.S. immigration policy away from its racialized and restrictionist focus on European immigration and changing the demographic profile of the United

4. Olson, "Whiteness and the Polarization of American Politics," 709.

5. Thomas Piketty, *Capital in the Twenty-First Century,* trans. Arthur Goldhammer (Cambridge, Mass.: Belknap Press of Harvard University Press, 2017); see also Dani Rodrik, *Straight Talk on Trade: Ideas for a Sane World Economy* (Princeton, N.J.: Princeton University Press, 2017).

6. For more on the challenges of secular stagnation, see Sarah Brouillette, Joshua Clover, and Annie McClanahan, "Late, Autumnal, Immiserating, Terminal," *Theory and Event* 22, no. 2 (2019).

7. Amelia Thomson-DeVeaux, "America's Social Safety Net Wasn't Ready for the Coronavirus," *FiveThirtyEight,* April 8, 2020.

States.[8] Indeed, the growing economic inequality and stagnation of the neoliberal era have at times been both offset and obscured by the enhanced opportunities of communities that were legally excluded in earlier eras—namely, African Americans, women of all races, and various communities of color. Today, it is communities that have suffered historical exclusions that offer evidence that the United States remains a space of opportunity and upward mobility.

This combination—a legal transformation away from Herrenvolk democracy, a shift in the dynamics of U.S. immigration policy, and a massive upward transfer of wealth away from middle- and working-class Americans—is occurring in the historical context of a nation whose civic identity has long been enmeshed in the politics of whiteness and white supremacy.

Migrants and Movement: Scarcity, Domination, and Foreclosed Futures

Given this confluence of historical and economic forces, it's no surprise that today, a people who defined freedom through a violent and racialized sense of movement and futurity would view mi-

8. Of course, while the Hart–Celler Act led to increased migration from Asia, Africa, Latin America, and the Caribbean, the legislation also contributed to our current dysfunctional immigration process in relation to Latinos, particularly Mexicans. Hart–Celler imposed the first cap on immigration from the Western hemisphere (North, Central, and South America), drastically reducing the number of legal options for entry and creating new, arbitrary legal quotas on Mexican and other Latin American migrants. See Douglas S. Massey, Jorge Durand, and Nolan Malone, *Beyond Smoke and Mirrors: U.S. Immigration Policy in the Age of Economic Integration* (New York: Russell Sage Foundation, 2001); Mae Ngai, *Impossible Subjects: Illegal Aliens and the Making of Modern America* (Princeton, N.J.: Princeton University Press, 2004); Philip E. Wolgin, "The Immigration and Nationality Act of 1965 Turns 50," Center for American Progress, October 16, 2015; Tom Gjelten, "The Immigration Act That Inadvertently Changed America," *Atlantic*, October 2, 2015.

grants with an intense mix of envy, impotence, and rage. Because today, it is *migrants* who are on the move, struggling against the forces of limitation, fleeing violence, crossing borders, claiming opportunity, and transforming their futures through movement. Resolute in their efforts to fight for new futures where they can prosper and thrive, today, it is *migrants* who are widely recognized as engaged in an epic quest for freedom—a group understood to be risking their very lives to begin anew and claim opportunity for themselves and their families. For nativists who understand the right to cross borders with impunity as a prerogative of whiteness, seeing unauthorized migrants depicted in such world-historical terms is particularly galling. It's fundamental to the nativist worldview that Mexicans and other Latinx subjects should be both removable and disposable—seeing these subjects wield and exceed the law to achieve freedom and escape repression and subjugation is intolerable, especially with fellow citizens viewing such efforts with sympathy and/or admiration.

Indeed, nativists view such actions as a brutal assault on their own futures. Trapped in a zero-sum conception of resources and unable to envision practices of movement into territory outside their own Herrenvolk practices and desires, citizens drawn to the politics of whiteness can imagine cross-border movement only as a form of dispossession and violent domination. Limited by a scarcity logic in which migrant flourishing means citizen hardship, nativists in the thrall of whiteness presume that migrant movement will invert the practices of white democracy, causing whites to "lose their country." Trapped in their own fears and fantasies of domination and racial terror, nativists can't help but conjure Latinx migrants as subjects planning to inflict a vengeful politics of invasion, replacement, and *reconquista*.[9]

9. David Kelly, "Vision That Inspires Some and Scares Others: Aztlan," *Los Angeles Times*, July 7, 2006.

The Great Replacement: Hate Crimes and the Politics of Invasion

As scholars such as Leo Chavez and Otto Santa Ana have shown, threat narratives of replacement, conquest, invasion, and infestation have circulated for well over a century.[10] What *is* new is how this racist rhetoric is being promulgated by a particularly influential set of forces that includes a white nationalist president, a formidable conservative media ecosystem, and an empowered anti-immigrant and alt-right political contingent, often undergirded by a persistent gun culture.[11] Together, this nativist assemblage has taken up the white nationalist rhetoric of the "great replacement"—a conspiracy theory in which white people are being systematically "replaced" by people of color through mass migration (possibly orchestrated by Jews and other "globalists").[12] Fox hosts Tucker Carlson and Laura Ingraham in particular characterize white Americans as being "replaced through immigration to the benefit of Democrats." Ingraham tells Fox viewers that "the Democrats want to replace many of you . . . with newly amnestied citizens and an ever-increasing number of chain immigrants." Asserting that "foreign citizens will be electing our political leaders" and characterizing Democrats as "the party of foreign voters now," Carlson describes Democrats as engaging in "demographic replacement," using a "flood of illegals" to create "a flood of voters for them." Speaking to Fox's disproportionately white and elderly viewers, Carlson has asserted that he is not "against the immigrants" but rather "for the Americans," because

10. Chavez, *Latino Threat*; Otto Santa Ana, *Brown Tide Rising: Metaphors of Latinos in Contemporary American Public Discourse* (Austin: University of Texas Press, 2002).

11. See Zack Beauchamp, "The El Paso Shooting Isn't an Anomaly. It's American History Repeating Itself," *Vox,* August 6, 2019; Southern Poverty Law Center, "Hate Groups Reach Record High," February 19, 2019; Andrew Exum, "America's Gun-Culture Problem," *Atlantic,* March 5, 2018.

12. Courtney Hagle, "How Fox News Pushed the White Supremacist 'Great Replacement' Theory," Media Matters for America, August 5, 2019.

"nobody cares about them. It's like, shut up, you're dying, we're gonna replace you."[13]

Pushing a conspiracy theory that Democrats are encouraging noncitizens to vote to win elections, Trump, Fox, and other anti-immigrant forces have created a xenophobic resonance machine that continually characterizes Mexicans and other Latinx populations as an invasive force. Speaking to Texas lieutenant governor Dan Patrick, Ingraham characterized Texas as "completely overrun by this illegal invasion" and said that "calling it anything but an invasion at this point is just not being honest with people."[14] Trump has described an "invasion" of the U.S.–Mexican border "at least 21 times in public speeches, remarks, and campaign rallies in an eight-month period"; at a May 2019 campaign rally in the Florida panhandle, the president "used the word 'invasion' seven times in less than a minute."[15] In an effort to mobilize voters for his reelection through fear of a catastrophic takeover by immigrants, Trump's 2020 campaign purchased thousands of ads on Facebook that included the word *invasion*.[16]

At times, Trump's rhetoric reaches an even darker, more dehumanizing register. On June 19, 2018, he tweeted, "Democrats are the problem. They don't care about crime and want illegal immigrants, no matter how bad they may be, to pour into and infest our Country, like MS-13. They can't win on their terrible policies, so they view them as potential voters!"[17] Repeated characterizations

13. Hagle; Greg Price, "Fox News's Audience Almost Exclusively White as Network Faces Backlash over Immigration Coverage," *Newsweek*, August 10, 2018.

14. Hagle, "How Fox News Pushed the White Supremacist 'Great Replacement' Theory."

15. Alexia Fernández Campbell, "Trump Described an Imaginary 'Invasion' at the Border 2 Dozen Times in the Past Year," *Vox*, August 7, 2019; see also Aaron Rupar, "Trump Turns Shooting Migrants into a Punchline at Florida Rally," *Vox*, May 9, 2019.

16. Thomas Kaplan, "How the Trump Campaign Used Facebook Ads to Amplify His 'Invasion' Claim," *New York Times*, August 5, 2019.

17. Abigail Simon, "People Are Angry President Trump Used This

of migrants as an inhuman "infestation" threatening America's very survival may help explain why a twenty-one-year-old white Texan would drive ten hours to an El Paso Walmart, where he would carry out a mass shooting that killed twenty-two people and injured twenty-four others. Telling the police that he was "targeting Mexicans," the El Paso shooting was one of the deadliest hate crimes ever committed against Latinx people in the United States.[18] In a manifesto posted to the online forum 8chan shortly before the attack, the shooter echoes the rhetoric of Trump and Fox News hosts and contributors, stating,

> This attack is a response to the Hispanic invasion of Texas. They are the instigators, not me. I am simply defending my country from cultural and ethnic replacement brought on by an invasion. . . .
>
> Due to the death of the baby boomers . . . and the ever increasing Hispanic population, America will soon become a one party-state. The Democrat party will own America. . . . They intend to use open borders, free healthcare for illegals, citizenship and more to enact a political coup by importing and then legalizing millions of new voters. . . .
>
> Statistically, millions of migrants have returned to their home countries to reunite with the family they lost contact with when they moved to America. . . . This is an encouraging sign that the Hispanic population is willing to return to their home countries if given the right incentive. An incentive that myself and many other patriotic Americans will provide. This will remove the threat of the Hispanic voting bloc. . . . This will also make the elites that run corporations realize that it's not in their interest to continue piss off Americans.
>
> My whole life I have been preparing for a future that currently doesn't exist. The job of my dreams will likely be automated. Hispanics will take control of the local and state government of my beloved Texas, changing policy to better suit their needs. They will turn Texas into an instrument of a political coup which will hasten the destruction of our country.

Word to Describe Undocumented Immigrants," *Time,* June 19, 2018; Michael Harriot, "All the Times Donald Trump Tweeted the Word 'Infested,'" *Root,* July 29, 2019.

18. Alexia Fernández Campbell, "The El Paso Shooter Told Police That He Was Targeting Mexicans," *Vox,* August 9, 2019.

> America can only be destroyed from the inside-out. If our country falls, it will be the fault of traitors. This is why I see my actions as faultless. Because this isn't an act of imperialism but an act of preservation.[19]

I quote this historically inaccurate racist screed at length not only to illustrate its Herrenvolk logics but to highlight how the logic of white supremacy has stunted and deformed America's political imaginary. Echoing the history of the Texas Rangers, Border Patrol, and paramilitary militias, the shooter approaches the border as a site where one can act with impunity. Moreover, as a white subject, the shooter understands himself as possessing not only a natural right to self-preservation but a natural "right to violence."[20] And like earlier conceptions of the frontier, traveling to the border to engage in mass murder was, for the shooter, an act of "frontier freedom"—a chance to engage in a civilizational struggle characterized by retribution, sacrifice, and domination.[21] For the El Paso shooter, Mexican suffering and death represent a form of deterrence, part of a larger effort—one that includes Trump's violent practices of raids, detention, and deportation—to diminish or do away with the "Hispanic voting bloc" and drive them back to their "home countries."

Divided Whiteness and the Democratic Imaginary

As scholars of whiteness remind us, white identity has left a tragic and lasting mark on the American democratic imagination.[22] Emphasizing standing and status rather than political partici-

19. Carmine Sabia, "Here Is the El Paso Shooter's Entire Purported Manifesto," *Federalist Papers,* August 3, 2019.

20. Grandin, *End of the Myth,* 54; Rogin, *Fathers and Children,* 42.

21. Grandin, *End of the Myth,* 116.

22. Olson, *Abolition of White Democracy,* 128; James Baldwin, *The Fire Next Time* (1963; repr., New York: Vintage, 1992); Toni Morrison, *Playing in the Dark: Whiteness and the Literary Imagination* (New York: Vintage, 1993); Morrison, "Mourning for Whiteness," *New Yorker,* November 13, 2016.

pation and collective action, white citizenship continually constrains the meaning of both democracy and political freedom.[23] Articulating a passive conception of freedom, the white imagination views freedom as "something to possess rather than an activity to practice."[24] Moreover, as Joel Olson astutely observes, "perhaps the most insidious aspect of the white imagination is that it presumes that the system of rights and representation established in the Herrenvolk and post–civil rights eras is the highest political form attainable."[25]

Rather than envisioning a multiracial democracy in which we engage in collective forms of self-rule characterized by freedom, justice, plenitude, meaningful work, solidarity, justice, pleasure, and joy, Herrenvolk logics can envision democratic citizenship, freedom, prosperity, and popular sovereignty only through racialized narratives of deprivation, humiliation, exclusion, suffering, and removal. Rather than envisioning and enacting a better and more beautiful world, white democracy's vision is defined by scarcity. In the logic of racial replacement, nativists imagine social goods within an economy of exclusion and democratic forms of denial; there is no sharing of power; there is only one majority "taking control" from the other. In the white nativist imaginary, there is no expanding or inclusive vision of membership. Latinos being present and holding power marks the destruction of the nation, a "political coup."

Yet despite all the suffering and violence that the Herrenvolk imaginary generates, nativists cannot reverse the reality of America as a multiracial democracy—or erase visible manifestations of that reality. The United States has, and will continue to have for years to come, a rapidly growing Latinx population, both immigrant and native born. With the decline of its foreign-born share, the steady growth of the Mexican-origin population "is

23. Olson, *Abolition of White Democracy*, 129.
24. Olson, 127.
25. Olson, 128.

maintained entirely by the birth of US-born individuals," creating a Mexican-origin population that is young, growing, and not about to be removed or disappeared.[26] Notwithstanding Republican efforts to suppress voting and Census participation, the native-born Latinx population will continue to grow, migrants will continue to enter the United States, and their U.S.-born children will continue to lay claim to America's future.[27]

Equally important is that fewer white citizens embrace an ideology of whiteness and white democracy. Indeed, whiteness is becoming increasing salient at the same time that it is increasingly divided and pulling in different directions. As Alcoff reminds us, it is "whites themselves" who are "increasingly politically polarized on a number of critical issues," from guns to health care to race.[28]

Of course, in analyzing the growing ideological divide among whites, I don't want to ignore the pervasive and ongoing problem of whiteness and white advantage, nor do I want to downplay the shift in aggregate white partisanship. Trump was elected in 2016 because of the white vote: he won 58 percent of white men and women, whereas only 37 percent voted for Democrat Hillary Clinton.[29] Nevertheless, while there has been a clear defection of whites from the Democratic to the Republican Party beginning in the 1960s and 1970s, those white voters who *do* identify as Democrats are becoming increasingly liberal regarding questions of racism and racial justice.

As a 2018 report by the think tank Data Progress declared, "we're witnessing a historically unprecedented shift left in opinions about race among [white] Democratic voters." White Democrats "increasingly reject racism" and are "much less likely to endorse

26. Jiménez, "This Too Shall Pass," italics added.

27. Noah Bierman and David Lauter, "Trump Backs Down in Fight over Census Citizenship Question," *Los Angeles Times*, July 11, 2019.

28. Alcoff, *Future of Whiteness*, 10.

29. Alec Tyson and Shiva Maniam, "Behind Trump's Victory: Divisions by Race, Gender, Education," Pew Research Center, November 9, 2016.

individualistic explanations of racial inequality and are more supportive of structural explanations of racial inequality."[30]

In sum, we are seeing a growing rupture between white citizens who support the politics of whiteness and those white citizens who are increasingly averse to racist and xenophobic appeals to white resentment. The police killing of George Floyd in May 2020 has only accelerated and intensified this shift in racial attitudes. Across the United States and beyond, increasingly large numbers of white people participated in rallies, marches, and demonstrations, joining with Black, brown, and other nonwhite communities to show their opposition to racist policing. White protesters carried signs reading "Black Lives Matter," "Racism Is a Pandemic," "White Silence Is Violence," "Use Your Privilege to Opt In for Those Who Can Never Opt Out," "Socially Distance from Anti-Blackness," "Convict Killer Cops," and "Confront Your Racist Family Members."

In addition to the protests, over the course of just a few weeks, monuments to the Confederacy are being taken down in cities across the South, with officials planning to remove many more. The National Association for Stock Car Auto Racing banned the Confederate battle flag from its venues, and the state of Mississippi voted to retire its state flag—the only state flag left in the nation incorporating a Confederate battle emblem.[31] Across the nation,

30. See Justice Democrats, "The Future of the Party: A Progressive Vision for a Populist Democratic Party," April 2018. According to Alcoff, numerous surveys have shown that "about half of whites agree with most people of color on many issues related to race on issues like antiblack racism, immigration, and criminal justice." See Alcoff, *Future of Whiteness,* 9–10. See also Sean McElwee, "The Rising Racial Liberalism of Democratic Voters," *New York Times,* May 23, 2018; Matthew Yglesias, "The Great Awokening," *Vox,* April 1, 2019.

31. Nicholas Reimann, "Here Are All the Confederate Monuments Now Coming Down," *Forbes,* June 9, 2020; Michael Levenson, "NASCAR Says It Will Ban Confederate Flags," *New York Times,* June 10, 2020; Rick Rojas, "Mississippi Governor Signs Law to Remove Flag with Confederate Emblem," *New York Times,* June 30, 2020.

white Americans have been engaging in what has been described as a "wave of self-examination" that has included reading books about racism and anti-racism, watching films and documentaries about African American history, researching their ancestry to learn about family connections to slavery, discussing anti-Black racism and white privilege with nonwhite friends and colleagues, and arguing with family members.[32] And while it's too early to know if this moment will develop into a deep and sustained reckoning with the legacy of white supremacy in the United States, such actions mark a profound shift in how certain white citizens are engaging questions of race. In sum, white nativists' ability to engage in Herrenvolk practices is threatened not only by the growth of America's nonwhite population but by the changing nature of white identity itself.

Whiteness and the Taking of Rights

This divide regarding the meaning of whiteness—a topic that until very recently has gone undertheorized in American politics—has important implications for current debates regarding the "authoritarian turn" in American politics. In recent years, there has been a growing discussion regarding the Republican Party's increasing "disregard" for democratic norms. Current studies by political scientists have been arguing that America's constitutional democracy is being endangered by what is often described as an "authoritarian turn," "asymmetric polarization," "hyperpartisanship," and "incipient fascism." Such assessments are not wrong, but their analyses will remain limited and inadequate until they situate this antidemocratic behavior within a longer trajectory of white supremacy and Herrenvolk democracy.[33] White supremacy *taught*

32. Amy Harmon and Sabrina Tavernise, "One Big Difference about George Floyd Protests: Many White Faces," *New York Times,* June 12, 2020.

33. Steven Levitsky and Daniel Ziblatt, *How Democracies Die* (New York: Broadway, 2019), and Jason Stanley, *How Fascism Works: The Politics*

white citizens to see themselves as both the defenders and beneficiaries of liberal democracy, claiming the rule of law while disregarding democratic norms and stripping subjects of rights in order to seize and retain power. Theorizing whiteness and the politics of white standing is fundamental to understanding why today's GOP is reluctant to defend—or openly hostile to—the expansion of the franchise, majority rule, a free press, judicial independence, and the safeguarding of constitutional protections.

Herrenvolk democracy's deep ideological and historical resources connect citizens who remain invested in white democracy to a politics that sees legitimacy in denying rights not only to people of color but to the white citizens who are now also "anticitizens." For nativists and the Right, their opponents are not fellow citizens so much as an "un-American left-wing mob" that includes "the radical left, the Marxists, the anarchists, the agitators, the looters." In his July 3 speech at Mount Rushmore, President Trump characterized such people as engaged in a "merciless campaign to wipe out our history, defame our heroes, erase our values, and indoctrinate our children."[34] Calling them "bad, evil people" whose beliefs are "completely alien to our culture," Trump suggested that such subjects can never be incorporated—they can only be vanquished.[35]

of Us and Them (New York: Random House, 2018); see also Norm Ornstein, "Yes, Polarization Is Asymmetric—and Conservatives Are Worse," *Atlantic,* June 19, 2014; Max Boot, "America Now Has a Party of Authoritarianism—It's the GOP," *Washington Post,* December 11, 2018; Paul Krugman, "The GOP Goes Full Authoritarian," *New York Times,* December 10, 2018; Zack Beauchamp, "The Republican Party versus Democracy," *Vox,* December 17, 2018; George Packer, "The Corruption of the Republican Party," *Atlantic,* December 14, 2018; Jennifer Rubin, "The Descent of the GOP into Authoritarian Know-Nothingism," *Washington Post,* February 17, 2020.

34. Remarks by President Trump at South Dakota's 2020 Mount Rushmore Fireworks Celebration, Keystone, South Dakota, July 4, 2020.

35. Remarks by President Trump at the 2020 Salute to America, Washington, D.C., July 5, 2020.

The Trump administration's July 2020 assault on predominantly white protesters in Portland, Oregon, vividly exemplifies this dynamic. Characterizing the mostly white supporters of Black Lives Matter as anticitizens—"anarchists and criminals" who "hate America"—the acting director of the U.S. Department of Homeland Security sent federal agents into Portland as part of "rapid deployment teams" that included two thousand officials from CBP and ICE.[36] Dressed in camouflage body armor and heavily armed, often with no visible identification, federal agents assaulted protesters, sometimes engaging in "abduction-style" detainments, pulling demonstrators into unmarked vans.[37]

It should have surprised no one to see federal agencies, with broad support from GOP officeholders, redirect these officers from violently apprehending and abusing migrants to attacking mostly white protesters engaged in antiracist protest and civil disobedience. Nor should we be shocked that the political party most invested in whiteness would be willing to disregard democratic norms in its effort to seize and retain power.

The ability to render certain populations rightless, to deny members of the community equality under the law, and to see them only as an undeserving threat—while still seeing themselves as lawful and honorable—*that* is the tyranny that lies at the heart of white democracy. The authoritarianism that threatens our democratic ideals is more than Trumpism or some newfound willingness of Republicans to shatter norms. It is the grasping desire of the Herrenvolk.

36. Sergio Olmos, Mike Baker, and Zolan Kanno-Youngs, "Federal Agents Unleash Militarized Crackdown on Portland," *New York Times,* July 17, 2020.

37. Mike Baker, Thomas Fuller, and Sergio Olmos, "Federal Agents Push into Portland Streets, Stretching Limits of Their Authority," *New York Times,* July 25, 2020.

Acknowledgments

The number of colleagues and friends whose feedback and suggestions helped improve this project is beyond the space I have available here to mention. But those who took the time to read and talk with me about it I cannot thank enough.

Writing about anti-migrant violence and the participatory politics of white cruelty had not been the plan. Prior to the 2016 election, I had been researching not white nativists but Latino conservatives. Like many other scholars at the end of the Obama era, I saw the politics of neoliberal multiculturalism as an entrenched and ascendant phenomenon—even among Republicans. I was interested in analyzing the political challenges and possibilities that occur when Latino conservatives invoke their race and gender identities to articulate their conservative worldview. At the same time, like other Latinx scholars inspired by the immigrant-rights movement, I was writing and teaching about how migrants had been organizing, resisting, and claiming rights in the context of increased xenophobia and ongoing criminalization.

What I failed to anticipate was how a deep desire to reassert whiteness would lead conservatives to spurn pragmatic multiculturalism in favor of a white nativism they found more viscerally satisfying. Following Trump's election and the immediate and aggressive targeting of migrants, I realized that before I could make sense of Latinx conservatism, I needed to understand the status of migrants within this overwrought and emboldened nativist imaginary. This book is the result.

I am grateful to the following institutions for their hospitality and generative feedback: the University of Washington's Institute for the Study of Ethnicity, Race, and Sexuality; Fordham

University's Workshop in Social and Political Philosophy; the American Studies Workshop Series at Princeton University; and the Junior Faculty Speaker Series in the Political Science Department at the University of Michigan.

I am especially appreciative of two invitations I received while working on this project: that from Joe Lowndes and Debra Thompson, whom I thank for inviting me to participate in the Race and Politics Workshop at the University of Oregon, and that from Mary Louise Pratt, Renato Rosaldo, and Felipe Gonzales, to whom I am grateful for inviting me to join the Advanced Seminar Program at the School of Advanced Research in Santa Fe. Both multiday workshops put me in conversation with a community of scholars whose feedback was truly transformative.

I also want to thank Pieter Martin at the University of Minnesota Press for his enthusiasm for this project and for shepherding it to completion and Joe Lowndes for his invaluable suggestions and feedback on the manuscript.

I was lucky to work on this project in many locations—Los Angeles, London, Montréal, Reykjavík, Bozeman, Portland, Edinburgh, Santa Fe, and New York—and with travel paused, I am constantly reminded that when it comes to finding joy, who you're with matters more than where you are. With that, I dedicate this book to my husband, Matthew Budman, whose support and invaluable editorial feedback always push me to sharpen my language and claims. Thank you for being not only the love of my life but the best quarantine buddy ever.

(Continued from page iii)

Forerunners: Ideas First

N. Adriana Knouf
How Noise Matters to Finance

Andrew Culp
Dark Deleuze

Akira Mizuta Lippit
Cinema without Reflection: Jacques Derrida's Echopoiesis and Narcissism Adrift

Sharon Sliwinski
Mandela's Dark Years: A Political Theory of Dreaming

Grant Farred
Martin Heidegger Saved My Life

Ian Bogost
The Geek's Chihuahua: Living with Apple

Shannon Mattern
Deep Mapping the Media City

Steven Shaviro
No Speed Limit: Three Essays on Accelerationism

Jussi Parikka
The Anthrobscene

Reinhold Martin
Mediators: Aesthetics, Politics, and the City

John Hartigan Jr.
Aesop's Anthropology: A Multispecies Approach

Cristina Beltrán is associate professor in New York University's Department of Social and Cultural Analysis. She is author of *The Trouble with Unity: Latino Politics and the Creation of Identity.*